A Festschrift for
Ian Hamilton's
sixtieth birthday

Limited Edition

First published in Great Britain in 1999

by Cargo Press
Tregarne, Manaccan,
Cornwall, TR12 6EW.
UK

© this collection of essays Cargo Press.

ISBN
1899980 06 7

A CIP catalogue record for this book
is available from the British Library

Acknowledgments

Cargo wishes to thank
all the contributors for their generosity and cooperation,
and Robert McNab for the end paper photos of Ian's desk,
Patricia Wheatley for the photo of Ian on page 8,
Julian Barnes for the cartoon 'Pillars' on page 40
that first appeared in Clive James' *Peregrine Prykke's Pilgrimage*
Through The London Literary World
Colin Falck for the cartoon from *The Review* on page 128
Russell Davies for permission to use both,
Hugo Williams for the photo 'Girls Girls Girls' on page 80
Farrar, Strauss and Giroux for permission to use Michael
Fried's poem 'Pain' from his *To the Center of the Earth,*
New York, 1994,
Picador for its permission to use Karl Miller's piece,
from his autobiography *Dark Horses,*
London, 1998
And Faber & Faber for the quotations from Ian's poetry.

Our thanks to South West Arts
for their assistance.

ANOTHER ROUND AT THE PILLARS

Essays, Poems, & Reflections

on

Ian Hamilton

General Editor
David Harsent

Cargo Press

Contents

Editor's Acknowledgements

A number of people have helped during the compiling of this book, but none more so than Derrek Hines, publisher of Cargo Press.

Introduction

Personal reminiscences aside (the confirmation of rumours, the scotching of rumours, new rumours begun) the two principal aspects that emerge from this festschrift are Ian Hamilton's work as a poet and as the editor of two literary magazines: *The Review*, and *The New Review*. This is not to sideline his work as a biographer and essayist – his biography of Robert Lowell, alone, demonstrates the importance of those undertakings – but to confirm that Hamilton the poet and Hamilton the editor work off the same impulse. That is, critical stringency: the notion of excellence.

Having a strong, and strongly defended, critical attitude doesn't, I think, dictate the means by which poems are written, but it does produce the climate in which they're written. It's what feeds you; it's the air you breathe. Hamilton's poems are about as far from doctrinaire as you can get. Indeed, as one of the 'miraculous persuasion' he is, in some ways, more given over to instinct and serendipity than many. However, it's clear that the body of work he's produced proceeds, in part, from convictions that hold good for all poems: nothing comes easy; it's possible to tell a good poem from a bad one, and say why.

The fact that *The Review* and *The New Review* were, at the same time, so well regarded and so vilified had precisely to do with Hamilton's uncompromising critical line. Reputations were made, enemies were made, no prisoners were taken. Now, twenty years after *TNR* folded, that kind of critical rigour simply isn't to be found. Not even a body of opinion. Everyone, it seems, knows everyone else; everyone rubs shoulders; and while some badmouthing might go on over the lunch table or at the party – a murmur, a wry downward glance, a hiccough of laughter – there's an air of timidity about the place that prevents divisiveness, prevents debate. Timidity – the enemy of passion.

What this means, of course, is that we need a *New New*

Review, but I guess we're not going to get one – not least because however much a magazine might pick its friends and pick on its foes, belligerence, while a good start, isn't enough; well, isn't anything without other qualities to back it up. When you look at *TNR*, you find those other qualities at once, qualities that anyone who knows Hamilton might expect: intolerance of the phoney and second rate, a sardonic sense of humour, a refusal to compromise, an insistence on intelligence and discrimination alongside a belief in the instinctive possession of 'a good ear'; but, more than anything, a tireless commitment to the art of poetry that meant fostering real talent every bit as much as exposing the fakes.

To talk of the indivisibility of editor and journal might seem obvious (it should be, but it's not); in this case, however, the style and tone of the thing were unmistakably the style and tone of Ian Hamilton. This festschrift celebrates that style and tone: in the poems, in the magazine, in the man.

David Harsent
October 1998

The Bitter Lemon Days

The term 'Fleet Street' will soon need to be marked *obs.* in dictionaries; while its parasitical sub-community of Grub Street has already shrunk to a Gissing title. The dispersal of newspaper offices to the newer, cheaper fringes of the City, plus the introduction of filing by fax and modem, means that a certain kind of literary-journalistic fraternising has died out. Of course, writers and journalists still meet; parties go on; clubland survives; the new kids necessarily conspire against their seemingly sclerotic yet endlessly cunning elders; but a geographical focus has disappeared. When I first came to literary London in the mid-1970s, you did not have to be either sober or fit to walk the boundaries of an area which enclosed *The Times* and *The Sunday Times*, *The New Statesman* and *The Spectator*, *The Observer* and the *TLS*. *The Guardian*, stuck up in Farringdon Road, seemed an exotic distance to the north.

Within this zone there were certain fixed points: Gaston's, where review copies were sold, and where suitcase-bearing literary editors tried not to coincide visits with their own deputies carrying mere spongebagfuls of surplus literature: the Bursa Kebab House, the Casa Alpina, the Bung Hole, two branches of El Vino's, various sandwich bars, greasy spoons and subsidiary pubs. Shuttling between these place of recreation and the literary editors' offices were a succession of freelances, bellettristes, hacks and hopefuls. Characters such as Maurice Richardson, ex-pugilist and Surrealist novelist, tipsy and terrifying, rather like a louche Randolph Churchill, with an instinct for the weakest point in a magazine office: the weakest point (as I discovered when it was me) being the person he could persuade to authorize a cash advance against some future set of short notices. Or John Coleman, proud contributor of more work to *Cambridge Poetry* than Thom Gunn; who wrote two pornographic novels for Maurice Girodias before settling down to a life of elegant film criticism; who sunbathed on the roof of *The New Statesman*'s Great Turnstile building, yellowed his white beard with Gauloises, and who would be punished if, for some reason (usually the usual one), he failed to make his required length, by a teasing entry in the contributors' box: 'John Coleman is the author of *The Enormous Bed* (Olympia Press)'. There existed a loose sense of connection to previous Bohemias, to Fitzrovia and Bloomsbury, back to the original Grub Street, whose inhabitants Johnson defined as 'writers of small histories, dictionaries, and temporary poems'.

The most westerly point on the literary map was Greek Street, home of *The New Review* and the Pillars of Hercules, not that they seemed especially distinct. Both were presided over by the chief Temporary Poet of the region and subject of this tribute. At that time there were a number of remarkable literary editors around, a fact contributors took for granted, little realizing that this state of affairs was rare and, as far as newspaper editors and proprietors were concerned, not particularly desirable. Nowadays a literary editor tends to be someone once caught with a hardback propped open in the office canteen, and constantly under pressure to turn literature into news stories. Then a literary editor was a stylistic and even moral influence on the whole paper. At *The Observer*, whenever something vulgar or dumbing-down was planned, they waited until Terry Kilmartin took his holidays before implementing it, rather than be shrivelled by a frown and a groaned 'Oh my God'. At *The New Statesman* the front half was jumpy about the back half's scorn of ill-written pieces. Still pervasive there was the influence of Karl Miller, the only person to have edited the royal flush of literary pages – *The Spectator*, *The Listener*, *The New Statesman* – with *The London Review of Books* still ahead of him. The third of this formidable triumvirate was Ian Hamilton.

All three had alarming reputations. Kilmartin's style was

kindly-schoolmaster, though you were aware that after fixing your dishevelled copy he would return home to the real work of retranslating Proust. Miller was known as an editor who, after dense silence, would with a gnomic question point up the quite shameful idiocy of your main contentions. Hamilton, though, was held to be even more frightening. He could be as silent as Miller, and when he did speak was as terse as his own poems – and boy, were they terse. Actually, he did not so much speak as let a few ironic syllables escape captivity from the corner of his mouth. He was as gabby as James Coburn in *The Magnificent Seven*, as vivacious as Charles Bronson in that and every other movie; as deadly as the pair combined. One Famous Writer brought him a piece and wisely absented himself to the Pillars while Hamilton read it. On his return Old Stoneface told him that if torn into small pieces it might serve adequately as cat litter. 'Fine, fine,' replied the FW, 'May I borrow your phone?' Whereupon he rang his office and began chewing out his secretary. It made perfect psychological sense. Hamilton not only had terseness and high standards on his side – there was also a streetfighter element to him. He stared people down in pubs. He offered to go outside with them if they wanted to prove their point. Hamilton drank all day and was never seen the worse for wear. Oh, and another thing: he never paid you. He told you your stuff was marginally OK, printed it with pained regret, and then sent you a cheque which bounced.

All of this terrified me. I was new to literary London. I had bought myself a bottle-green velvet suit, because the uniform of young littérateurs in those days was supposedly velvet. I wore it to a party at *The New Review*. 'Is that your literary London suit?' someone asked, not unkindly, but as if I were sporting L-plates on my trousers. And then there was the drinking. I had a very light head in those days, and after a single drink would retreat into taciturnity; two and I would be mute for the rest of the day. This wasn't the best help to my career. Worse, my choice of liquor in those days was gin and bitter lemon. The first time Ian offered me a drink in the Pillars and I told him what I wanted, he didn't react, no doubt confident that he had misheard me. When my unbutch choice was confirmed, he frowned like Housman confronted by a textual error in a new edition of *Manilius*. He was still generously willing to stand me the round, but unable to pronounce every word in case the barman got the wrong idea. 'Large whisky, pint of Old Skullsplitter, a gin and … you say it.' 'Bitter lemon,' I admitted, completing the order and my shame. Later we had lunch. I like lunch. Dinner too. I ate everything on my plate. I had very little money, after all (there were only two sorts of contributors at *The New Review*, those who could afford not to be paid, and those who had no money anyway and so wouldn't notice the difference if they weren't paid). Ian looked at my scoured and bread-swabbed plate with benign contempt. His own was still piled with food which had undergone brief, sardonic rearrangement. He lit another cigarette. I didn't smoke at all in those days. 'You want another gin and what was it?'

Perhaps it was my hopelessness with the arriviste's camouflage that softened him; at any rate, he never turned his petrifying asperity on me. I don't like to inflict retrospective damage on his reputation, but he was very, well, nice to me. This may make him sound like a gin and bitter lemon, but it's true.

He was encouraging, he would buy me drinks as long as I spoke their name, and he would pay me. I was probably their poorest contributor at the time – though I realize many contend for this title; certainly I was way below the tax threshold. But *The New Review* operated on ad hoc anarcho-Christian principles. Craig Raine, when books editor, commissioned Lord George-Brown, as he either was or later became, to review Solzhenitsyn. The phone rang. 'Lord George-Brown's article is ready for collection from the House.' 'Can you tell him to put it in the post?' The review arrived, was conscientiously rewritten, and duly appeared. A while later the phone went again. 'Lord George-Brown's fee for his article is one hundred and fifty guineas.' 'Well, our fee,' Craig replied, 'is nothing, love.'

After the try-out of a book review, Ian asked me to write the *Edward Pygge* column. News, publishing gossip, light interviews, with what felt like a vast space to fill each month. He sent me off to interview Harold Acton, Edna O'Brien, Joan Didion, Elizabeth Smart and that dread poseur George Barker. Some of these interviews were a bit sticky. Edna O'Brien relaxed me with the line, 'You can place your tape-recorder just there, young man.' I had to admit I didn't have a tape-recorder. This was *The New Review*, after all. As we proceeded, it became clear that I hadn't come to do the Big Interview on the grown-up pages, but the quick snooty para at the back of the mag. A certain unease established itself. Finally, I made the mistake of quoting the Weidenfeld blurb of her new novel, which compared it to Dostoevsky and Camus. 'So you don't agree with it, then?' she asked huffily. 'I'm sure Camus would have liked my novel.'

Ian put me on the masthead. Contributing Editor. 'It's just a way of not paying you,' was the interpretation of a cynical chum. But this wasn't the case. It made me feel as if I had real existence, as well as superior status. I realized that all those guys hanging about the office looking like poets, wondering whether Ian would like to come out for a drink, being incredibly cool and behaving as if the days were there for the frittering (most of them were Hugo Williams), weren't really doing all that – they were just waiting to be paid. I felt protected. I felt a bit less so when I attempted to chastise a moderately well-known writer in my Greek Street column. A few years previously he had edited an anthology featuring a number of better-known names (Empson is one I remember). Skimming a second-hand book catalogue, I noticed many of their original typescripts, plus supporting correspondence. Inconceivable that Empson and Co had each simultaneously flogged to the same dealer their typescripts and their returned letters. I made the obvious comments about editors' perks. I may even have mentioned theft. Ian told me the para would have to go. For legal reasons, I assumed. Since I'd recently read for the bar, I enthusiastically explained our can't-lose defence. Ian shook his head, a minimalist gesture at the best of times. 'Friend of the magazine' said the corner of his mouth. Ah. The Mafia tone implied that it might be foolish to enquire what 'friend' actually meant.

But then 'friends' counted the more because there seemed a lot of enemies around Ian. The usual personal ones which every poet acquires by choosing that fratricidal literary mode; but also institutional ones. The notion that a literary magazine might receive an Arts Council subsidy was regularly denounced in the press. The fact that *The New Review* was a large-format glossy and not printed on recycled Bronco was an extra offence. No doubt the grim financial self-consciousness favoured by more pro-saic businesses was a little lacking. But in fact the magazine was sustained far less by public money than by the devotion of an impoverished staff. Most literary magazines are like this, of course. However the devotion at *The New Review* was considerable. Hugo Williams recently rang me up for a quote about Ian. 'What do you need ?' I asked. 'Perhaps you could say something like, "He was the Gaffer".' I didn't then, but on reflection I will. He *was* the Gaffer, and what this means in literary journalism is: someone whose presence and example make you write as well as you are able.

This isn't a straightforward matter. There are many kinds of literary editor: those who gush and flutter; those excruciatingly tortured at the idea of running into a real live contributor; those who imagine that being frostily unresponsive is a sign of integrity and cool. This last category have mislearnt the lesson of Kilmartin, Miller and Hamilton. The trick is not a lowering silence, but a concentrated reading of the text followed by exactly targeted blame or praise. It sounds easy, put like that, but it isn't. As a writer, you like literary editors for their praise, but you trust them for their blame, for identifying weak spots in your piece which you half-knew existed but were half-refusing to admit.

At that *New Review* party, by now thoroughly embarrassed in my literary London suit, I found myself next to Hans Keller. This must have been in 1978, I suppose. He shocked me by saying that he was going to vote for Mrs Thatcher next time, as a protest against Labour's 'irresponsibility'. He meant their fiscal irresponsibility, and I wonder what he thought of the alternative he helped vote in. I also wonder what he thought of the fiscal responsibility or otherwise of *The New Review*. Most of us couldn't have cared less about that. What makes you want to write for an editor is their moral and literary responsibility. So here's a toast to the Gaffer, in whatever juice you prefer. Which reminds me that it was while I was delivering copy to Greek Street that I met Robert Lowell for the only time. In the Pillars of Hercules, naturally. And do you know what he was drinking? Bitter lemon, as it happens. Without even the gin in it. I trust that's in your biography, Ian?

Missing Person: In Search Of Ian Hamilton

Ian Hamilton is a double act, or a series of double acts: savage critic and lyric poet; Soho *bon viveur* and suburban recluse; commanding presence and modest absence. How to make sense of this? In part, it's that his various roles aren't as contradictory as they seem: in everything he puts his name to – the biographies, anthologies, longer essays, shorter reviews and occasional (but never Occasional) poems there's a consistent and distinctive tough-mindedness. But it's also that, as he has found new ways to live and write over a longish career, bits of him have been discarded or gone missing or no longer express themselves as they once did.

Certainly anyone born after 1970, say, might easily miss the fact that he was once, round the age of thirty, a shaping spirit, acclaimed and even revered as *the* poet, editor and critic of his generation. To recover a sense of this, you have to look back to the final issue of his magazine *The Review* in 1972, and its symposium on 'the state of poetry'. Clive James: 'I am compelled to wonder if any magazine has ever done such a good job of evolving and applying tests of falsity in poetry.' David Harsent: 'As it would be unnecessarily coy to avoid the point, I might as well say that *The Review* seems to me to have been responsible for fostering much of what is best in English poetry at present.' Colin Falck: 'When *The Review* was started in 1962 it was in the slightly arrogant hope of being able to concentrate the weight of our major poetic tradition – up to and including, say, Lowell and Larkin – behind the work of new poets .... Perhaps the most important thing to say about these poets (Ian Hamilton, Michael Fried, Hugo Williams) is that they have begun, over the past decade, to forge an idiom which looks flexible enough to deal with any experience the modern world is likely to come up with. The slightly laboured diction of Hamilton's earlier poems has given way to a rhythmic control unequalled in contemporary verse ... If we call this ten-year-old development a movement it could yet turn out to be the most important one since early-twentieth-century modernism and perhaps (because less entrammelled in irrelevant theories) more radical than that.'

It's true that all these writers were intimately associated with *The Review*. But it wasn't the kind of magazine that went in for sucking up. Hamilton could allow himself to print stuff like this because he'd already made a mark, not because he needed to. The trenchancy of *The Review* was acknowledged far beyond Oxford and London. The distinctiveness of its school of poetry had been much remarked on – already, two years earlier, Anthony Thwaite had produced a pastiche of a typical *Review* poem. Like him or not (and some didn't), Ian Hamilton was where the action was.

Yet for someone so omnipresent, he could also be, even then, very elusive, as I became aware in the early 1970s, while researching a thesis on post-war English poetry and fiction. Advised to consult *The Review*, by then defunct, I turned it up in the Senate House library in London, found it both useful and stylish, and bought up as many back copies as I could. Ian Hamilton was named as editor, on the inside right hand page, and I could sense him hovering over several contributions (most ostensibly those of 'Edward Pygge'), but signed essays and reviews by him were rare. Undeterred, I took out a subscription to *The New Review*, just launched in 1974. His name was there again, as editor, and his voice whispered between the lines, but the only articles by him were about famous literary editors of the past. Still searching, I bought *A Poetry Chronicle* (1973), but found the poetry and life it chronicled that of others, not his own. I also bought his one collection of poems, *The Visit* (1970), and liked its spareness, but thought it enigmatic to the point of impersonality. Beginning to think of him as Godot, I met men who swore he existed and claimed to know him, among them Karl Miller (who took over thesupervision of my doctoral thesis in 1975) and Craig Raine (who in 1977 became books editor of *The New Review*.) Finally, in 1978, came a breakthrough. I'd been reviewing for *The Times Literary Supplement* and *New Statesman*, and now Craig Raine sent me a batch of novels to do for *The New Review*. I read them, wrote the piece, submitted to Craig's editing, corrected the galleys and waited: soon, surely, I'd be invited to the office and get to meet the man himself. But the phone call, when it came, was to say that the piece wouldn't after all be published (which I'd half-expected) and that I couldn't be paid (ditto) because *The New Review* had folded, which I hadn't expected at all. I felt bereaved more than aggrieved. I'd missed my chance.

As it turned out, I did visit *The New Review*'s office some months later, in the company of Craig, Tom Paulin, Christopher Reid and David Sweetman. A rare diary entry of mine records that we met in the Pillars of Hercules, the place packed out with Scots down for the England match – you had to knock on the doors to get in. After the pub, and a meal nearby, we bought wine at an off-licence and, with nowhere else to go, drank it in the dead office of *The New Review*, to which Craig had still a key. We were all pretty drunk, with Tom – who kept saying 'I like London' – disinclined to return to Nottingham. One of the few sensations I do clearly remember was that of trespass, as we sat swigging wine around Ian Hamilton's abandoned editorial chair. No doubt, young poets being competitive, not to say parricidal, there was a sense of usurpment, too: weren't we the new generation, partying in the mortuary of our predecessors? Maybe we were: four of the five of us were alleged members of the Martian school, and Craig's subsequent spell co-editing the magazine *Quarto* gave us a platform.

24

But both *Quarto* and the Martian school were short-lived. Besides, Ian Hamilton wasn't a Big Daddy we wanted to kill off, but a poet and editor we admired, and, at a mere *40*, hardly an *éminence grise*. If I imagined him at all that day in his empty office, it was as a condoner (and enabler) of our drinking, debate and gossip – a generous absence, not a hostile one. Another diary entry suggests I finally met him a month later, at a Friday *New Statesman* lunch, in the company of Martin Amis, Julian Barnes and several more. These Friday lunches were pretty drunken occasions, too: I spent most of one puking in the Gents, not man enough to stand the pace (and they were invariably all-male affairs). The diary is too terse for me to tell whether the puking happened at this lunch, or a later one, and has nothing interesting to say about Ian Hamilton, either: even sober, I would have been too starry-eyed, meeting Godot at last, to have my wits about me.

   I told myself it was his serious-mindedness I looked up to, but doubtless part of the attraction was that *The New Review* was, or had been, rather chic. Its shiny format and imaginative use of cover photographs seemed to say that contemporary writing could be sexy, commercial, even fashionable – an unfamiliar notion in the drab late 70s, before Waterstones arrived and made it true. In those unglamorous days, there were loud complaints, mostly from writers, about the size of the Arts Council grant which *The New Review* received. In the title essay to *The Trouble with Money,* Ian Hamilton recalls his ordeals in front of the Arts Council's literature panel: 'Wild-eyed anarchic novelists would transmute into prim-lipped accountants. Tremulous lyric poets would rear up like tigers of the bottom line. Book-reviewers who, I knew, lived in daily terror of being rumbled by the Revenue were all at once furrow-browed custodians of *public funds*.' Something austere in me, too, recoiled from *The New Review*'s luxuriance. Perhaps in some small way I even contributed to its demise. In June 1978, in a piece for the *TLS* about little magazines, I'd complained that *The New Review* seemed to be less interested in poetry than *The Review* had been, and wondered if this was because its editor had become disillusioned. Ian Hamilton doesn't usually write aggrieved letters to newspapers, but next week came a sharp rejoinder protesting that he was as interested in poetry as he'd ever been. As the editor of a magazine under threat of losing its grant, he had to say that. But I think he meant it, and that I was wrong. As well as Craig Raine and Christopher Reid, *The New Review* published poems by Sean O'Brien, Andrew Motion and Tom Paulin, none of them at that time well known. To be interested in poets younger than yourself is one of the great tests for editors and reviewers who write poetry themselves. Ian Hamilton passed it.

Looking back at *The New Review* twenty years on from its demise, I'm struck by how many other tests it passed, too. It encouraged not only young poets but young fiction writers: Ian McEwan is the prime example, but I remember also enjoying a story called 'Annie, California Plates' by the previously unpublished Jim Crace. *The New Review* engaged with the issues of its day – from apartheid, the Soviet empire and terrorism to psychiatry, semiotics and Public Lending Right (to which it devoted most of one issue). It was bold with its covers: one 'double issue' carried a photograph of David Hockney and R B Kitaj standing naked together – in 1977 it was no small thing to put a penis (let alone a pair of penises) on the front of a mainstream cultural magazine. It was fiercely loyal to the writers it loved, notably Robert Lowell, about whom Hamilton later wrote his best biography. It had provocative essayists in Colin Falck, John Carey and Jonathan Raban, and *The Review* pages were outstanding. And at a time when newspapers didn't go in for them, it found room for long literary profiles and/or interviews (Barthes, Larkin, Iris Murdoch, Anthony Powell, Beryl Bainbridge), as well as enterprising bits of reportage (Mark Kidel's 'The Hip Capitalist Dream' was surely the first investigative piece about Richard Branson), occasional play-texts (including Pinter's *No Man's Land*), and a gossip column, Greek Street. *The New Review* missed its moment: 10 years later, in a more buoyant and risk-taking economy, it would have prospered. To read its 50 issues again is to realise how badly we lack an equivalent monthly today. There is *Granta* (a quarterly), and weekly books coverage in most newspapers and magazines. There is *The New Yorker* and there is *Prospect*. But there is nothing like *The New Review*.

To launch a literary magazine and keep it going requires certain qualities: an appetite for new writing; high critical standards; a shrewd understanding of the previous literary generation; an ability to inspire one's peers, or energise them, or at any rate to get them to write for you without offering much financial return. As an editor, Ian Hamilton had all these qualities, much as Ezra Pound did, but he lacked Pound's cocksureness and didn't go in for manifestos. His critical manner was sardonic and deflationary. Most poems failed to impress him, his own included. He published those he thought good, but didn't kid himself they were better than they were. He was serious without being earnest – the cover of *Fifty Poems* makes him look parsonical, but his was a worldly, chain-smoking version of Leavis and Matthew Arnold. He was confident in his critical judgments, but he was not arrogant, and felt uncomfortable with the role of He Of Whom Great Things Are Expected. Nothing got past him – least of all himself.

Another way of putting this would be to say that, behind the famous toughness (mocking eye, boxer's nose, corner-of-the-mouth disparagement, fag in one hand, drink in the other), he was shy – a man happier in the shadows than in the limelight. He can't exactly have minded people saying that he was *the* poet/critic/editor of his generation but he seems to have had little appetite for any attendant publicity. Not that the age of PR had fully dawned on poetry then, but many a lesser talent has become a celebrity by exploiting this level of attention. Hamilton's preferred role was more rueful – not defeated exactly, but not excitable either. Some of his best friends were rich and famous (or have since become so), but for him the literary life meant rent arrears, spent advances and coffee jars filled with pennies – the pram in the hall and the bailiff at the door.

When bailiffs are at the door, you escape them by disappearing or hiding your identity – by assuming anonymity. Ian Hamilton picked up a trick or two of this kind at *The New Review*, which was habitually in financial trouble. He'd also learnt about anonymity while working at *The Times Literary Supplement* at a time when the reviews were famously unsigned. Later he wrote about JD Salinger, curious to know why a writer at the height of fame should cease publishing his work and go into hiding. More recently, he has explored the forces that made Matthew Arnold abandon his lyric self and adopt the mask of school inspector. Unfulfilled promise is one of his favourite themes (it's why Cyril Connolly interests him, too), but beyond this lies an uncommon fascination with the way in which writers move between two poles: self-expression at one extreme, self-effacement at the other. Though not as violently as Salinger or Matthew Arnold, he has himself struggled between these same poles. 'Staying true to himself' as a poet has brought near-silence. Even when vocal, he's hardly forthcoming. For somebody with such a strong presence, there is also a curious absence about him.

The idea of absence is inescapable when you read his poems: the absence of all the poems he might have written instead of the bare sixty he has; the absence in the poems he has written of the stuff of his life (as he himself asks: 'The raggedness of every-thing, the booze, the jokes, the literary feuds, the almost-love-affairs, the cash, the somehow-getting-to-be-forty and so on: where does all that show itself ?'); the absence in the poems that

plainly *are* about his life of the people that mean most to him, who
are now dead ('From my corner pew/I command an unobstructed
view/Of your departure'), or have disappeared ('It's almost twenty
years/Since I last saw you', 'You are not with me, and for all I
know/You may not have survived'), or who even when present are
ill, distracted, not themselves: 'Your eyes are open/But you're far
away...' ; 'You have forgotten almost everything/We promised never
to let go'; 'You're small, and smaller still/With every move you
make'.

Absence can sometimes speak volumes – slim volumes,
anyway. In Ian Hamilton's case, it can also make the reader's heart
grow fonder: there being so little to treasure, we treasure what there
is all the more. His poems are too guarded to be called candid
but they are certainly emotional. Hamilton once described them as
concentrating on 'the intense climactic moment of a drama', and
the drama usually involves a man watching over a woman suffering
mental breakdown or emotional distress. Happier moments are
confined to the past, or foresee their (unhappy) expiry. There is
nothing in the hauntingly beautiful poem, 'Old Photograph', to
tell us that its lovely moment is irrecoverable, but surely it is.

> You are wandering in the deep field
> That backs on to the room I used to work in
> And from time to time
> You look up to see if I am watching you.
> To this day
> Your arms are full of the wild flowers
> You were most in love with.

This is Hamilton at his most minimalist: seven lines, with
no rhyme scheme or metre, only three adjectives ('deep', 'full',
'wild'), and the barest punctuation (just two full stops). Describing
a photograph, the poem seems to record a single moment. Yet

we're told that 'from time to time' the woman looks up, which in a photograph she couldn't do: the poet has reinhabited not just the moment captured in the shutter, but other moments surrounding it, during which the woman checks to see if she is being observed – not by a neutral lens but by a lover's eye. There's a vulnerability about this gesture of hers, a need for reassurance, which is felt again in the final image of her holding flowers: we know these flowers she is 'most in love with' will fade and die, as the love felt for her may also die, but in the photograph she and they and it are painfully alive still. It's a desperately simple poem, but there is nothing simple about the desperation (the sense of loss and longing) which underlies it. Nor are the particulars of its you-and-I vignette quite so local at they seem. The woman's arms are 'full', and the poet's heart is full, and the poem is full of resonance, in part because of affinities with Eliot's hyacinth girl in the first section of *The Waste Land*:

> when we came back, late, from the hyacinth garden,
> Your arms full, and your hair wet, I could not
> Speak, and my eyes failed.

Poets divide into camps: there are leavers-out and there are putters-in. Ian Hamilton is firmly in the first category, but his poems, for all their brevity, don't feel niggardly. They may hoard their meanings, but you'd guess, even if you didn't know, that the poet himself is not a hoarder but a spendthrift. Despite the miserliness of his output, there's the off-page presence of a largeness, and *largesse*: as well as the few words that are said, there's the pressure, in the margins, of all the words that might have been said, given the chance.

A sure grasp of what should go and what's worth keeping is part of what makes Ian Hamilton an unforgiving critic: he is finely attuned to the various wrong notes (self-importance, superficiality, melo-drama) which a poet can strike. He can be too severe at times: he is when he describes Larkin's 'A Large Cool Store' as 'a rather silly poem about nighties', and he is when he accuses Ted Hughes (of whose work he has been wilfully unappreciative) of 'skimped and shallow dealings with the human world'. But at least his severity is consistent: he isn't soft on friends' poems (see 'Critique': 'me with your dud manuscripts/face downward on my knee'), nor on his own. Indeed, he's at his most unforgiving with himself: hence the meagreness of his output. 'Early on I had shots at getting "more of the world" into my verse,' he says, but he decided that he was better off (or at) doing the inclusive thing in prose. For myself, I wish he weren't quite so austere, and didn't feel the need 'to keep the whole business of 'my poetry' quite separate from the rest of my so-called literary life.' But it has to be admitted that the two poems of his which don't make such a separation – 'Larkinesque', about a session in the divorce court, with nods to 'Dockery and Son'; and 'The Forties', about being a middle-aged 'father of the house' – are so strained and self-conscious as to suggest his policy is probably right. These two poems make wincing use of quotation marks time and again – 'wrap it up', 'strictly Socratic', 'evening stroll', 'organic greens' – with an embarrassment that keeps us, and the narrator, at a distance from the experiences described. The early poems are very different: locked inside some moment of crisis, they use quotation marks only to record things people have actually said, and though these things can sound portentous and implausible ('By these analogies we live' doesn't sound like real speech to me, nor 'My blood excites this petal dross'), at least there's no ironic self-awareness to break the spell. Ian Hamilton's later poems are worldlier, but seem more doubtful of their right to exist

Why Ian Hamilton gave up editing is no mystery: he'd done it for nearly two decades, needed a change, and fancied a slightly less onerous way of making a living. Why he has given up writing poems, or at any rate publishing them, is harder to say. Some poets suddenly find it impossible to write poetry in middle age. Some write at the same rate as they always did but, unhappy with the results, destroy them or lock them away. A few lose sight of the *raison d'etre* for writing poetry: Matthew Arnold did, as is made clear in Ian Hamilton's biography, certain sentences from which may apply to his own case. For example: 'As [he] came to see it, an all-out commitment to his art would have involved an "actual tearing of one's self to pieces". It might also have involved some other kinds of damage – to people, to principles, to his ingrained sense of social purpose.' Or: 'what the age didn't need were more poems of the kind [he had] a real gift for, and indeed had already written: lyric poems of the self, that ... self which, as he came to believe, had or should have had more important things to do than, well, write lyric poems.' In truth, I doubt whether Ian Hamilton believes there are more important things to do than write lyric poems. More likely, since he's not the same man who wrote the lyrics of *The Visit*, he may doubt whether he's the right person to do the job. It's a pity, if so. He may be a different kind of poet now, but he has the talent still, and it's not too late to use it. If his sixties bring more poems than his thirties, forties and fifties did, some of us will be quietly cheering. His prose books, however good, are no consolation. In poetry, he has been a missing person for too long.

A Alvarez

Ian Hamilton

Ian and I first met in 1960 when he was 'president, chief executive and general mastermind of the Oxford University Poetry Society'. That is how he described himself in his wicked *New Yorker* profile of Stephen Spender, and I suppose it's a miracle that we ever saw each other again, given what he goes on to say about the lessons he learned as boss of the OUPS:

> The week before Spender's visit, we had dinner with
> W H Auden ... The week after, we would be getting
> Robert Graves. Why these grand figures put themselves
> to this inconvenience - no fee, no audience to speak of,
> and a dinner that few of them ever seemed to
> touch remains a mystery to me. But it was rare for a
> poet, however famous, to turn down our invitation.
> One or two of them, unbelievably, came back for more.
>
> In retrospect, I can see that this was my
> introduction to the limitless vanity of poets: they'll put
> up with anything provided that they get to read their
> works.

Maybe I got through Ian's net because there was no way I qualified as 'grand'. I wasn't famous, I had no back-list at that point – one book of criticism and a couple of pamphlets of poetry – and, anyway, I was far too young – thirty years old to his twenty-two. Eight years may have seemed a lot when we first met, but it rapidly became nothing at all, particularly after Ian founded *The Review*, in 1962, and began to publish things of mine in it. The relationship of editor to contributor is a great equaliser, no matter how small a fee is involved.

As it happens, we became close friends and have met every month or two ever since. Ian, in fact, is one of only two or three good friends of mine who actually write for a living and, because

I have become less sociable over the years, he is now my sole link to the literary world. He dislikes its vanity and follies as much as I do, but he is stuck with it professionally. Once a literary editor, I mean, always a literary editor. Ian, unfortunately, is no longer in charge of a magazine, but he still seems to feel that it is his duty to know who's who in Grub Street. Or maybe everyone in Grub Street wants to know Ian because his standards are so high. Certainly, the fact that we have continued to meet makes me feel obscurely pleased, as if I had passed a difficult test.

The truth is, Ian is a hard man to please and almost impossible to fool. He has a beady eye for whatever is phoney or sentimental. This combination of shuddering distaste for overstatement and a sure instinct for clear, emotionally precise language gives his reticent poetry its strength; he has made an art of looking away without disguising the price you pay for doing so. The same qualities also make him a formidable literary critic, although they mean that, on his scale of values, nobody escapes whipping. Mention the name of any prominent operator in the lit. biz and Ian's sardonic mouth tightens, his eyes glint and somebody's done for, his or her vanity fatally skewered with a joke. I have never for a moment kidded myself that Ian doesn't see right through me, too. I simply assume that he is willing to overlook my failings because he likes me.

To be fair, he is even harder on himself than he is on other people. Recently, we were talking about his mother, who is old and ill and miserable. 'If my life were like hers, I'd rather be dead,' Ian said. 'Come to think of it, if my life were like mine, I'd rather be dead.' He was only partly joking. For as long as I've known him, he has been engulfed in disasters, most of them financial. He has also steadily refused to extricate himself from them, as though he believed that making an effort on his own behalf were morally distasteful, a gesture that might somehow be construed as self-promotion rather than self-help. He has written eloquently on

The Trouble With Money – it is the title essay of his latest collection – but his particular trouble with money is not that he is above it but that it has always been above him. At the start there may have been 'a near-priestly kind of romance in the idea that a high purposed literary career would be profitless, at least in terms of cash', but that didn't last long. He had the usual middle-class habits – he smokes, he drinks, he likes to eat out – and he swiftly acquired the usual middle-class responsibilities of a family, a mortgage, alimony. He worked hard to support them all, but his heart wasn't in it. It was in poetry, the least profitable of all the arts, and no matter how solemnly he pretended otherwise, he couldn't take money seriously. But money is like the godhead – it never manifests itself to those who don't truly believe in it – so the disasters kept on coming and kept on getting worse. There may be one or two people who know as much as Ian about contemporary poetry, but I can't believe that any living writer is more expert on how to cope with creditors, bailiffs, Inland Revenue auditors, the Official Receiver and the bankruptcy court. It must be a nightmare for him but, from the outside, the whole show has come to seem so much out of control that it is laughable. Or almost laughable. As Adlai Stevenson said when Eisenhower beat him a second time, 'I'm too old to weep and it hurts too much to laugh.'

As each new calamity rolls in, Ian reports on it deadpan, with a high critical impartiality, like a theatre critic at a dreadful farce at which he is not a participant but a helpless spectator like you. He can't beat it, so he might as well make fun of it, and he is an effortlessly funny man. For me, in fact, one of the great pleasures of his company is that he makes me laugh more or less all the time. And not just about literature: for example, when I told him my daughter was working for the man who invented virtual reality, he replied, without missing a beat, 'How can she tell?' Mostly, however, the jokes are at his own expense. Another example: a meal with Ian goes on for hours. It is like a science-fiction experience in which time implodes, waiters age before your eyes and generations of diners come and go, while Ian toys disdainfully with the food on his plate and ends up eating almost nothing. I'm the opposite: I'm greedy, I wolf my meal and often end up eating his, too. Once, when I had long finished and he was being more dilatory than usual, I asked him if he minded if I smoked while he was eating. He looked at me in amazement. 'Mind?' he said. '*I* smoke while I'm eating.'

Ian's nose for literary talent is as spectacular as his lack of financial success. As editor of *The Review* and *The New Review,* he was the first to publish all sorts of writers who went on to become rich and famous: Julian Barnes, Ian McEwan, Jim Crace, Clive James. While they moved up in the world, he stayed broke and the bailiffs moved in and his magazines folded. But not even the most inflated ego would seriously claim to have more literary taste and intelligence than Ian Hamilton. There is a moral in that, but I prefer not to draw it for fear of making him cringe.

Andrew Motion

Philip Larkin met Cyril Connolly once, at John Betjeman's Memorial Service. 'Sir,' said Larkin, bounding forward (out of character and out of keeping) to seize Connolly by the hand: 'You formed me!'

Every writer, in every generation, has a hero-magazine. For Larkin in Coventry during the late '30s, it was *Horizon*. For me in Oxford during the early '70s, it was *The New Review*. (It would have been *The Review* if I'd been five years older.) All the other young writers-in-the-making I knew – they felt the same. The first time I met Craig Raine, in the Upper Reading Room of the Bodleian Library, he rolled up to me – 'D'ya wanna ... a cup of tea?'– speaking low and mean from one side of his mouth. At the time I thought he might have been offering me a really interesting drug, or speaking in code about my appointment on Boot Hill. Subsequently I realised it was just (just?) an impersonation of Ian. But I got the point all right. Maybe if we learned to talk like him, we might get published by him.

It was the mixture of heady austerity (the enigmatic compression of its poems) and an unnerving but familiar tone (in those stories by Ian McEwan, especially) which made the magazine so appealing. Everything felt exemplary in its discipline, but also possible and within reach – as if, given the right conditions, and a following wind, and a bit of growing up, it might be possible to place a poem there ...

I had the same sort of mixed feelings about Ian's own poems. On the one hand they were extreme – tight dramas of illness and distress – and extremely pared down. On the other, they had a surprising lushness – almost a poeticism: that 'swart fly'; 'The ice/That catches in your hair melts on my tongue'; 'I watch the blossoms break/ Beyond this gravel yard'. It all made for a strange set of contradictions – a poetic voice at once withdrawn and confiding, sarcastic and warm. It left me feeling simultaneously braced up and relaxed.

As things turned out, my poems did appear in *The New Review* before they came out anywhere else. By this time, my efforts to characterise Ian's voice for myself – as editor and poet – had settled into something pretty straightforward. I just thought that if he said a poem was OK, it *was* OK. Then more time passed, and this simple sentiment became complicated again. Partly, of course, thanks to meetings and friendship. Like a lot of over-awed young tyros, my earliest memories of our encounters are all embarrassing – to me. Especially the first one of all: a lunchtime rendezvous at the Pillars of Hercules, at which I arrived feeling the straw fairly sprouting out of my turn-ups, not knowing what to drink but sure beer would be too un-cool, spirits too expensive (I was still writing my thesis, and living on a grant), and wine – well, all right, provided it looked as though I was taking it seriously. Which led to the awful humiliation of a litre bottle (a *litre*) standing in front of me like a non-vintage blush, attracting Ian's unspoken but all-too-clear scorn while I tried to make myself sound interesting to him. Eventually (and indeed speaking out of the side of his mouth, but more consolingly than Craig and I had managed in our impersonations) he ushered me away to choose some books to review. I felt like a basket-case, led away from a terrible accident.

That's what I mean about 'becoming complicated again'. There was a mixture of scepticism and unlooked-for kindness in Ian that day, and it's the kindness I haven't forgotten. I think I see it now in a lot of his prose writing too – though what is 'kind' in company becomes something else in criticism. Take his long essay on Alun Lewis, for instance, which recognises the flaws in the work, its indulgences and swaggering, and its occasional voluptuous excess, but still admires the undertaking as a whole. Or again, more recently, with Matthew Arnold. Ian sees the fault-lines and limitations in the poems but still, without using any high-flown language of praise, allows them to live afresh in the world.

Andrew Motion

I saw someone, somewhere, writing about the Arnold book, saying it was a veiled autobiography: the story of someone who had pushed away lyric poetry (or had it taken from him), and turned to the busy world instead. It's true that Ian's admirers wish he wrote more poems. It's also true that his journalism is preoccupied by 'The trouble with money' and therefore by the question of how to preserve first poetic principles in a culture which won't take enough interest in their upkeep. But the comparisons end there. What Ian's new poems prove, and the Arnold book, and the recent essays, is the wholeness of everything he has done. The undergraduate self-portrait he sketches at the start of his essay on Stephen Spender – at once disarming and disarmed – is still recognisable. He has been true to the contradictions in himself. It means he goes on caring about the big, important things in literature – in poetry especially – and keeps writing about them with a properly tender toughness. Now as ever: if he says it's OK, it is OK.

Russell Davies Cartoon from *Peregrine Prykke's Pilgrimage*
Douglas Dunn, Ian Hamilton, Hugo Williams

Harold Pinter

Ian Hamilton

I first met Ian in the summer of 1960. He had invited me to see a production of a one act play of mine, *A Slight Ache* at, I think, Keble College, Oxford. He got me a room at The Mitre Hotel (long dead).

I was in my room at The Mitre (lots of wood) in the early evening. There was a knock at the door. It was him. He was very young. A great smile.

The production of *A Slight Ache* was very lively indeed. Ian had not directed it but he was responsible for the event, the producer, I suppose. He was pleased and proud. We had a number of drinks after the show. He then published the text in his magazine *Tomorrow*. This publication contained a classic typo: instead of 'slight pause' one read 'silent pause' – whatever the hell that might mean. However, 'silent pause' passed into the Methuen publication and various foreign translations until someone spotted it many years later.

I started to read Ian's poems later on in the Sixties and thought *The Visit* a quite beautiful collection. Those great opening lines:

> Miles off, a storm breaks. It ripples to our room.
> You look up into the light so it catches one side
> Of your face, your tight mouth, your startled eye.

And:

> At four, a line of trucks. Their light
> Slops in and spreads across the ceiling,
> Gleams, and goes

41

I read his poems at various public gatherings and was struck always by the audience's response to a poetry which was at one and the same time so delicate and so full of sinew.

There's another great and I think highly characteristic line in his last collection *Steps*. It's the last line of 'At Evening':

I'd talk to you about it if I could.

Can't believe he's sixty. I still see him framed in the doorway at The Mitre.

College Daze

At sixty it's with trepidation that you contemplate any writing involving memory of events distant in time, ironically in this case, the Sixties. Long ago I decided to keep diaries only for appointments and the odd *donné*. I've little means of verification, even of dates, because, thinking my memory reliable then, I didn't name or even enter every appointment. Now I doubt that accurate recall is possible. Trepidation is increased by finding that whenever Ian and I reminisce we frequently meet blank looks from each other over specific recollections. And finally, there is the danger of retaliation from your victim with superior memory power and or better records, especially those of a skilled biographer over those of a translator – occupations neither of us envisaged then.

Unsurprisingly I first met Ian in connection with the University Poetry Society. We were both in the last generation, after deferment, of those who were obliged to do national service. (It is his face I remember expressing shock at seeing some fresh-men, straight from school, playing tag in the High.) He'd been trained as a teleprinter operator, I think, hence his skill as a typist and, presumably, the dogged clinging to his manual typewriter. Two-fingered cack-handers like me were happy enough to go for erasureless print-outs, the avoidance of retyping, the inevitable correcting-fluid and marginal additions. Ian was a year ahead at university. I did hospital, instead of military, service and since my college place was delayed two years I'd decided to go up early and work at the Radcliffe Infirmary.

In those pre-college days I gate-crashed some of the Poetry Society meetings and came across Ian who seemed already to have something of a critical influence over some of the budding bards, partly because he edited his own magazine, *Tomorrow*. Robert Coleman Williams, Ian McLachlan, Stanley Golightly – already published in the *London Magazine* – and Clive Jordan were other names I remember. And another Ian, later Yann, Lovelock, my fellow Radcliffian and gate-crasher, whom Robert Coleman Williams once invited outside to be thumped over some vital issue of poetic quality. Anyway, he went Beat of his own accord. But without his neck I wouldn't have intruded, then diffident and shy to the point when it could seem to others like distance or arrogance.

My first college memory of Ian was of the Freshmen's Fair at which the Poetry Society used to try to fund itself for the year by drumming up members like mad who dropped out just as madly – or, probably, sanely. Over the public-address system, to attract would-be punters, he read Anthony Hecht's 'The Vow' with repressed, passionate conviction. This was hardly noticed. With some fury he announced he would read it backwards because nobody ever listens. And he did.

We were also linked by our connections with Oscar Mellor, painter, photographer, printer-publisher of the Fantasy Press, and – mysteriously, without university connexion – sort of *de facto* overseer of the Poetry Society. Ian lodged at Oscar's, I think, for a time. I remember a somewhat shaken Ian telling how he had stepped out on to the landing the moment that the ceiling of the room had caved in and smashed the typewriter. Ian's relations with Oscar – as with relations between most poetry-magazine editors and their printers – became somewhat strained. A projected Fantasy pamphlet of Ian's may have faltered more over Ian's perfectionism and unwillingness to publish than anything else. I suspect I was to some extent the unwitting beneficiary since Oscar sprang the chance of a pamphlet on me, presumably to fill the gap. But the manly Coleman Williams was Oscar's favourite poet.

Oxford's regulations were a bore: gowns, gate-fines, battels – the number of meat-pies you had to eat to graduate – a year's college residence, segregation of women, exeats to leave town in term, permissions for residence in vacs. Disregard for the last nearly got me sent down but that's another story. Marriage was discouraged by the reluctance of the authorities to award grants to married students. Some of us found their reluctance a handy reason for delay. Anyway, you made other arrangements as Ian and Gisela did. Pauline, my girl-friend, lived at Sandford. With money in short supply, since our town rooms had to be kept on, we both stayed up in the vacs. The girls worked locally and I worked shifts at the Radcliffe. What Ian did I forget but I don't think he took a job, at least never for long. Given the complications of life, including the three-mile cycle ride to Sandford, it was surprising how often Ian and I managed to meet.

At the time of the Cuban crisis a Trotskyite friend of Ian's, renting the room next door to him in 99 Woodstock Road, rushed off in Spanish War style to defend Cuba. Ian suggested that I take the vacated room. His poem 'The Recruits' was a reaction to the crisis.

I remember being surprised to see a vase of flowers in Ian's room and was told that Gisela had put it there to brighten the place up. This showed a gentler aspect to Ian which I should have noticed by then but had not. It rather shook me because Pauline would not have risked trying such a thing in my room. It would have been a concession to 'poeticism' and the vase would anyway probably have ended up being accidentally spilt. Ian's vase showed a naïve would-be sophisticate that it was possible to be a modern poet and like a flower or two.

Sadly, Woodstock Road brings memories of Jon Silkin who died as I was preparing this piece. He used to come up to sell *Stand* by main force about the university and stacks of the magazine gathered on the landing outside our rooms. Mrs Rose, our landlady – who would not accommodate girl-students because they were untidy – was always complaining of these piles and being reassured that Jon was coming to remove them. One morning I heard this complaint being uttered on the landing and opened my door in time to see Ian fling his wide to reveal Jon. Five-foot one, he fitted Ian's sofa comfortably and had slept through the racket until this moment. Needless to say the piles of magazines hardly diminished. Ian informed me that to save time it had been decided to boil the eggs in the electric kettle and make the coffee or tea from the same water – which perhaps showed an unusually practical side to his nature and is one of the few known examples of Ian ever cooking. As for his practicality in other directions, I'm still always surprised by 'The trellis that needs fixing, that I'll fix.'

An impractical side was revealed one morning when I encountered him on the landing with half a small loaf of stale bread in his hand which he had put out on his window-sill facing the back from which the five other gardens mentioned in 'The Recruits', could be seen. 'The buggers haven't eaten a bit.' It didn't seem to have occurred to him to crumble it for the birds.

But 99 can't have been an easy place for Ian in his final year. The house was full of mainly second-year students making hay. There was, unusually, a lesbian Trinitarian theology student smuggled in by the near-alcoholic David Hamill in the cell-like basement room. Alex Cockburn was on the first floor – visited by Jane of the generally acclaimed legs; opposite, Steven Itscovitz, researcher into lasers and David's drinking partner. On the ground floor was Clive Jordan, also in Ian's year, who wrote reviews for *Tomorrow* and *Agenda*. On occasion when all the women showed up the house must have rocked. And there was the usual student night-time typing of last-minute essays. – And speaking of nights, Ian regretted that you couldn't smoke while sleeping. Apparently he's now nearly mastered that art. To crown it all, Ian had a bout of flu during finals.

Unfortunately, though, my room, the largest and emptiest, was often the common-room. I got a better lock in the end, having set fire to the carpet with the electric fire in the struggle to eject a would-be habitué. The fire reminds me that once Ian set the back of his trouser legs smouldering by standing too close to his own fire.

The first editorial address of *The Review* was here at 99 and the piles of *The Review* remained beside *Stand* long after Ian moved out late in 1962 to Beechcroft Road. Having submitted a poem to Alan Ross at *The London Magazine* I received a rather bemused rejection letter from him mentioning that there was another poet at the same address and did I know him? He seemed to doubt there could be two of us in one place.

A Beechcroft memory was of arriving one afternoon to be encountered by Ian's benign bewilderment and puzzled amusement at a stray dog they appeared to have acquired by the dog's choice. Yeats, it's recorded, moved Pound up in his crazy zodiacal system, having discovered him feeding the stray cats of Rome. Jon Silkin, of the peaceable kingdom, somewhat surprisingly found the dog less easy to take. On our leaving, Jon from the street gave the beatitudinous, raised flat-palm farewell, endemic in the Sixties, and Gisela, grinning on the step behind Ian, without his being aware, gave a solemn parody in reply.

In my final year we met when we could but, amid the varied pressures, I was anxious not to plough my finals since a good degree would be, I thought, the likeliest route towards time to write. Roy Fuller has a couplet in 'Chinoiserie': 'I've tried to take care that being a poet /Didn't get in the way of my making a living.' But Ian's and my worries were the other way round. He, too, was having a hectic time establishing his freelance career, writing, lecturing and making sorties into literary London – with a camp-bed of mine that fitted in a duffel bag.

We occasionally met in a pub before Ian was due to give an extra-mural or WEA lecture. It was amusing to see an uncharacteristic reluctance on his part towards the scotch because he wanted to avoid having to go for a piss in mid flow or vice versa. A post-1965 memory of an intake problem is of a meeting in the Pillars of Hercules when Ian was exercised over whether it would be okay to take a bottle of wine to dinner at a teetotal friend's.

In thinking about this piece I managed to ferret out some of our uncollected early verse; depressing measures largely, not helpful reminders of our discussions, though I was amused to find a sonnet of Ian's and one of Michael Fried's. But then things became clearer. We hadn't discussed these poems with each other, but rather the general situation for poetry, and drafts of verse in process that would appear in our first books. – I still notice some of the joins in both books.

In Oxford around the opening of the Sixties it was too easy to publish poems. There were so many outlets: *Isis*; *Cherwell*; *Oxford Opinion*; *Gemini* – rather fugitive; *The Oxford Mail*, even; The Fantasy Press; Michael Horovitz's circus, *New Departures*, pushing performance; William Cookson's *Agenda*; and, yes, Ian's *Tomorrow* which he now considers his 'pre-literate' phase. And in case of emergency I had brought a dilapidated printing press up with me.

Having swanned around the town for so long I found it easy to place material and published too readily. Of course I can't stand the stuff now. Ian of course couldn't stand it then. What changes? – Certainly not the terrible.

While I was busy publishing my own rubbish he was busy publishing other people's. I forbear to mention names like Horovitz, Wollen, Sladen, McGough among them. It shouldn't have been too much of a surprise, then, to discover I was sharing a prize poem spot with John Fuller in the last *Tomorrow*. (If I remember, £1 - 10 each; a dish of spag. bol. was 12 1/2 pence.)

But I was surprised by one of Ian's choices of judge, Thomas Blackburn, who had never impressed me. – Neither of us then knew that this was our 'pre-literate' phase. Though Ian would say to me: but you, you bastard, never like anyone's [poems]. I set a good example. He was later similarly charged by others, with similar exaggeration.

Initially I'd acquired an impression, that later many others mistakenly found, of Ian as a somewhat off-putting figure. He, we, liked to wear black, then. Black duffel coats were almost *de rigueur*. But you don't see so much of your own blackness. He could appear distant and unforthcoming when maybe only preoccupied, doubtful or bored. His criticism seemed to be offered with such assurance that at first one felt it was based on intellectually sound and rigorously held criteria rather than the more human, imaginative, sensitive and intuitive intelligence from which it actually came. It took a few discussions and exchanges of drafts to discover this. It always seemed as if a badly written poem hurt him; that showing him one was almost an insult or moral failing. But I can remember worriedly puzzling over the contents of issues of *Tomorrow* trying to find the criteria that linked the poems – and feeling inadequate when I couldn't see a coherence.

Our discussions of each other's drafts were always of detail and never reached overall approval: the odd awkward phrase or rhythm – suggestion and counter suggestion for hours. It may have been a case of poets manoeuvring like porcupines mating but there was a shared conviction that real poems, the perfect utterances, were few and far between, that the chances of this or that one being absolutely right were remote. In his biography of Lowell, Ian has the wonderful phrase 'the imaginable moral power of perfect speech'. The poems that go through you like a blade of ice are not often those of students or of the ignorant armies clashing in the literary media.

The things we said seem fairly commonplace now. If you

need a second sheet, it'll be no good. Cut that. Cut it down. That rhythm's wrong. Junk that rhyme. That's not real. That's not genuine. Nobody says that. Never did we say: lengthen it. Ian did pay me the backhanded compliment of saying that I rhymed well – adding: but why? I'm pleased to note that he uses more rhyme again, not always where expected. Steps – in an interesting direction.

And talking of second sheets, his method of composition amazed me. Most poems, I think, he shaped in his head until something viable emerged for typing out. But if he changed or developed something, out would come that sheet and in go another. He must have used scores of sheets on some poems, many with only a line or two on them.

The Movement was the current thing but neither of us was much impressed, except with Larkin; the Beats, too, and performance poets were emerging much to our unenthusiasm; energetic Ted Hughes was impressively different from the caution of the Movement but left us with considerable doubts. Gunn seemed to offer something, though the toughie stance was a bit wearing and the form sometimes heavy. The Americans, Lowell, Roethke, Hecht, Snodgrass, Plath, seemed to offer the chance of something more viable in some way – 'feelingful', a favourite word of Ian's; and early imagistic, critical Pound was a good besom for sweeping away much debris. Roethke's 'The Lost Son' impressed both of us and he visited the Poetry Society. I remember him saying in the drinking session afterward: 'My little finger has more spirituality in it than the whole of Tom Eliot!' – waggling it with his other hand.

Roethke also struck a chord with us when in his reading, packed to capacity and more, he announced a title, saying: ' "I Cry, Love! Love!" – I got that from Blake but I cut it down a bit.' – By one 'love'.

I remember few things that occurred while Ian and I in turn were involved with running the Society. It was a custom for the committee to entertain the speaker to dinner before the reading. Sometimes there were more people at the dinner than the reading.

It was embarrassing when committee members excused them-selves after the dinner and we traipsed off to a meeting with only three or four in the audience. One visiting poet, asked over dinner what he most disliked on such occasions, remarked that he was irritated by chairmen who forgot his name during the introductions. At the meeting, the chairman appeared to forget this poet's name. No one knows now whether it was a genuine lapse. Ian can be very absent-minded but it could have been a fine example of his humour, so often quietly and wittily used for deflationary purposes.

Blackmur, a critic that interested us both, came to speak at the university and was invited to the Society. In his lecture to the university, attended by many of the English dons, he remarked that, as he was speaking on 'The Waste Land', his lecture would be con-structed in a form similar to that of the poem. I for one could not detect too much similarity. Blackmur was known to like Italian food and at the dinner in the La Roma where we could thus respectably order our staple-because-cheap spag. bol., we were amused when he announced spaghetti should be eaten Anglo-Saxon style and chopped his all up – into a form similar to 'The Waste Land' that this time we understood.

When preparing to publish *The Storms* I was going to dedicate it to Ian but he pointed out that he couldn't then review it. The problem was solved by my hiding his name in an acrostic in the half lines of a dedicatory poem in Anglo-Saxon metric, allowing him to be suitably underwhelmed. No one at the time taxed me with this dodge though my editor, Kevin Crossley-Holland, translator of *Beowulf*, cracked it, telling no one.

Ian also complained wryly that I had anticipated him to the title which he had been contemplating for his book.

I close with memories of a workshop for the Borough of Sutton LEA which I shared with Ian and Peter Porter on the 6th and 7th July 1972. In the afternoon discussion of the first day Ian parodied one of the hand-out chunks, the section of Eliot's 'Tradition and the Individual Talent' that begins: 'Poetry is not a turning loose of emotion', etc. Ian simply replaced the talismanic repetition of the words 'emotion'and 'personality' with a series of less and less plausible juxtapositions which showed without ado the flimsiness and infinite variability of that form of argument. The final afternoon session next day was for requests from the students for favourite poems to be read. One asked for 'Out of the Cradle Endlessly Rocking'. Peter and I passed up the invitation and Ian with impressive equanimity took up the task of sight-reading aloud the six pages – a long stint for a so-called minimalist.

Hugo Williams

I worked for Ian for a while on *The New Review* in the mid-Seventies at 11 Greek St, the building where *The Review* had previously had a floor. Soho was a very different place in those days – rougher, darker, seedier, cheaper, nicer. (It was also, before its expansion to 'West' and 'North' Soho, smaller.) In the hot summer of 1976 the streets were full of strippers darting from one club to another wearing only their costumes. I have a photo of Ian coming out of his doorway while a girl touts for business from the next door Carousel Club, under the words, 'Girls, Girls, Girls'. It is an inscription which could have applied equally well to his own office, where a great many well-educated young ladies were working on the magazine. I tried to find the doorway recently, but like the rest of old Soho, it had disappeared completely.

There were far fewer places to go to in Soho in those days, or fewer places we went to. If you were being taken out you went to Bianchi's in Frith Street, next door to the Bar Italia, where Elena then held court. Or you went to the Presto, or 'MK's' as Ian called it, because the manager looked like the actress Miriam Karlin. Bianchi's has long gone and Elena has moved on several times since those days – she is currently at L'Etoile – but the Presto is still there at the time of writing, the decor intact, the atmosphere of TNR unchanged. I've heard that Ian would occasionally take writers to a certain Chinese restaurant, where he always ordered omelette and chips. The story goes that the manager took this to mean that he had just come out of prison and must be getting a big gang together with the likes of Gore Vidal driving the getaway car and Norman Mailer as explosives expert. He couldn't resist asking Hamilton what he was up to, adding, 'Don't worry, your secret's safe here.' I think the story has more metaphorical than literal truth about it.

To begin with, on *The New Review*, I was supposed to be the magazine's arts editor, but Ian would only countenance the very best writers as reviewers and it became a thankless task trying to get through to, say, Tom Stoppard, for what amounted to babysitting money. I left messages with Miriam Stoppard, who was kind, but Tom never did get back to me. I was happier when Ian gave me £100 towards a motorbike and I became the magazine's motorcycle messenger (I later went professional). There was less competition on the roads in those days and I could get up to Al Alvarez's house in Hampstead in less than ten minutes.

It goes to show how badly I wanted to get my poems into the magazine, that I should have showed Ian one called 'Bar Italia', set in one of the few venues to have survived the changes. It was written to or for Lucretia Stewart, who also worked in the office at that time. ' This is how me met' it began, 'sheltering from work in this crowded coffee bar … ' Typically, Ian was more amused than affronted to be handed this prima facie evidence of our truancy. Making a mock-martyred face, he accepted the poem and still tells the story against himself with anguished relish.

If my preferred shelter was the Bar Italia, Ian's outside 'office' was always The Pillars of Hercules, a pub which is said to guard the true spiritual entrance to Soho, via Manette Street. (I don't know where the spiritual exit is. Perhaps you aren't supposed to remember.) This pub gave its name to a book about the period by Clive James, one of the magazine's regulars. 'There was a handful of good literary editors in London at the time,' he told me once, 'Martin Amis, Karl Miller and Terry Kilmartin among them. But none of them could beat Ian at casting a cold eye on your prose, drawing a line in the margin beside the bits he thought didn't work and waiting with barely concealed disdain while you fixed it on the spot, usually at the bar of the Pillars.' I remember Ian entertaining a young poet there who didn't drink. 'Why not for

God's sake'? Ian asked. 'It tastes awful and makes you feel bad,' explained the young man. 'Well none of us *likes* it,' said Ian.

Before starting the magazine, Hamilton had done a reading tour of America following the publication of his book of poems, *The Visit* and thanks to his carefully assembled list of susceptible English departments I was able to follow in some of his footsteps a few years later. The trick, he told me, was to write and say you were going to be in their area, that way they didn't take fright at the prospect of a foreign visitor and you could generally pick up a useful 'emergency honorarium' of about $200 without disturbing their budget. When I returned from my travels, notebook bulging with Americana, Ian was the one who encouraged me to write it up, gave me some of his own best jokes on the subject and printed my first efforts in the magazine under the title 'Bard on the Road'. It was by keeping his caustic editorial eye firmly in mind that I was able to make a book out of it, for which he also found me a publisher and agent. It was this book which started getting me the sort of work which keeps me going to this day.

Lucretia Stewart also had a hand in getting me to start the book (not to mention Xandra Hardy at Cape who made me finish it). The Bar Italia poem to her goes on, 'Then you would hold out your hand and say, / Well, where are your three pages?' and ends 'I haven't written them. One day I will. / Anywhere but here it might seem possible,' which seems a mite ungrateful now, considering how easy-going the atmosphere was at *The New Review*, despite its money troubles. The fact is that things did get written in and around that boozy, strippy Soho. There are plenty of writers around today who wrote the stuff then which would set them up for life.

The magazine finally ran out of Arts Council steam at the end of 1978 – or was it the recession which did for it? Only one year before The Comic Strip, that intrinsically Eighties group of comedians, started up on the other side of Soho in the Boulevard Theatre, an annex of Raymond's Revuebar, with my wife Hermine as between-acts chanteuse. Odd to think of them as part of the same period, but perhaps they were on either side of a cusp. In 1981 Ian wrote a piece in the *LRB* about these bad boys in which he speculated on their future – and, incidentally, on that of Soho itself, which has pretty much suffered his prophecy. 'It is hard to see how The Comedy Strip can make it without cleaning up and thinning out their best material. Already they are moving into the area of "alternative success". It need hardly be said that television will try to turn Alexei Sayle into Les Dawson.' Even Ian could not have predicted that seven years later, in the era of TV's 'The Comic Strip Presents' (and its many repeats), leading Comic Stripper, Rik Mayall, along with coevals Stephen Fry and John Sessions, would be appearing in the West End revival of *The Common Pursuit,* the play Simon Gray wrote (and re-wrote) about Ian and his set. (My brother Simon had been in the original cast and comes in for some fine taunting from Gray in his production memoirs.)

It would be hard to exaggerate the influence Ian had on the way poetry was written in the Seventies. Almost single-handedly, with his high intensity lyric poems and equally high intensity reviews, he hacked a way out of The Movement and we all followed gratefully in his tracks towards a particular kind of emotional symbolism which he more or less invented. This was unfairly known as 'minimalism' at the time, as if shortness was its main purpose, or as if, which in my case was nearer the truth, we were trying to skive in some way. Ian has satirised the style himself: 'If we were going to write about Vietnam, it would have to do with going into some field and picking a flower that would somehow faintly remind us of a look or a gesture that distantly might hint of a war in South-East Asia. But the poem would be about walking in the field.' However, his own marvellous short poem on the subject, 'Newscast', would be impossible to satirise in this way.

Once read, it is impossible to forget:

> The Vietnam war drags on
> In one corner of our living room.
> The conversation turns to take it in.
> Our smoking heads
> Drift back to us
> From the grey fires of South-East Asia.

Far from relaxing his minimalist grip in the intervening years, Hamilton has actually trimmed several of his poems still further. The ten-line 'Windfalls' (1964), when it reappeared in his 1988 Birthday volume, *Fifty Poems,* presented only its initial four-line fly metaphor, which moved it, strangely, away from neurosis and towards the apocalyptic. 'The Recruits', from the same period, loses three of its twelve lines, among them the once-admired but now no longer quite possible 'At the trees, loafing in queues, their leaves rigid; / At the flowers, edgy, poised.' How one had strained to get that 'loafing in queues' sort of thing in one's work. Now it was lopped forever.

The favour I found with Ian as editor in the early years of *The Review* was the first in my adult life and therefore, highly prized. Most of it depended on a poem about a butcher, which turned out to be about marriage. I remember thinking, ah, this is easy, now I'll go and do all the other shops. Somehow it didn't work out like that. Perhaps he was right and you can't go out looking for poems, you have to wait for them to come to you. 'If a poem isn't there,' he said in a recent interview, 'you'll never find it, no matter how hard you look. If it's not there, you can't invent it, however inventive you're feeling. This is a youthful notion, of being seized by poems, of being involved in a kind of miracle ....' I used to believe him and worried at my own grubbing instinct that put quantity first. Now I'm not so sure that his 'youthful notion' isn't a grown-up idea of a youthful notion.

I sometimes think that poems are a search for something which may or may not be there. You assemble your bits and pieces and you try to find if there is anything going on. As in any collaboration you can't be sure of the outcome. I don't know. It's sure you can't do anything much about the quality, but by going for quantity at least you stay ready.

It is a question Ian addresses in his new book, *A Gift Imprisoned: The Poetic Life of Matthew Arnold*. If Alfred Tennyson, the 'born' poet, was great, then he, Arnold, who had always been accused of forcing his talent, must be fabricated. Add to this Arnold's belief that enough poetry had been written already to satisfy 'religious wants' and you had a good case for shutting up shop completely. 'The book is about how far down you can adjust your idea of yourself without giving up altogether,' he has said, clearly referring to his own case. A misprint in the book's publicity handout lays it on the line: 'A Gift Imprisoned: The Poetic Life of Ian Hamilton'. The difference between the two poets being that Hamilton has not given up. In ' The Forties', the last poem in the 1988 collection, he wrote 'At forty -five / I'm father of the house and at dusk/ You'll see me take my "evening stroll"/ Down to the dozing lily pond...' It ends with the now famous image of resignation, 'The trellis that needs fixing, that I'll fix'. This looked at the time like a farewell, but today, on closer inspection, the poem seems to be more accurately about Arnold than Hamilton himself, who has recently published a pamphlet of new poems as good as any he has written.

Douglas Dunn

My first awareness of Ian Hamilton was in 1962. His magazine *The Review* was on sale in a Glasgow bookshop and I bought the first two numbers together. It was exactly the kind of criticism I needed to read. Believe it or not, but I sensed mischief in the forthright way Colin Falck, for example, in a review of *The New Poetry*, didn't refer to Mr Alvarez or Mr Anyone, but by surname only, pure and simple. In the same issue (No.2) Martin Dodsworth wrote of Mr Graves and also just Graves. Almost everywhere else it was Mr this and Mr that, Mr Leavis writing about Mr Eliot and Mr Eliot writing about Mr Leavis. But it wasn't excessive courtesy given the boot that excited me; it was the intelligent directness of 'Peter Marsh' and 'Edward Pygg'.

Shortly after that, Hamilton could be read elsewhere, in *The London Magazine*, for example, to which he contributed essays, as well as interviews with such poets as Philip Larkin. Later in the decade he could be read in *The Listener* under Karl Miller's editor-ship, and in other papers, such as *The Observer*. I used to watch out for his critical writing and for his spare and unyieldingly tender, acidically lyrical poems. By 1969 he was publishing poems of mine in *The Review* and the *TLS*, and it was around then or just before when I first met Ian, visiting him in Westbourne Terrace.

That both his parents were Scots put Ian at a bit of an advantage, I admit. I recognized the open smile and the nimbleness with which it was adjusted speedily to a sardonic and slightly puzzled off-grin – they were genetically instilled. Later on I discovered a very close resemblance between Ian's mother and mine, which Ian attributed to 'long-suffering'. As I recall, there was a moment of preliminary investigation into my credentials on my first visit to him. Nothing to do with poetry, the quick, genial testing was all about football. My first wife was with me. Having suffered a few nasty experiences on hockey fields, such as being obliged to play at all, she was very firmly of the belief that sport ought to be actively discouraged. Ian shuddered at this disclosure. But I think I passed the test, even if I've never been as obsessively interested in football as Ian continues to be. However, we have a pact. When I become what Ian calls 'King of Scotland', or what I call 'President of the Republic', then my first obligation is to make Ian manager of the Scottish team. Why anyone would want such a thankless task is beyond me, but as the prospect is so unlikely as to be animatedly ridiculous then this deeply serious pact, signed, as it were, in alcohol, can be permitted to run its natural course.

In 1971-72 Ian was Compton Lecturer in Poetry at the University of Hull, based in the Brynmor Jones Library, and following in the footsteps of Cecil Day Lewis, Richard Murphy and Peter Porter. Our usual routine was that I'd meet Ian off the train around noon on Wednesday, and then we'd go for lunch in a subterranean but decent restaurant in the Station Hotel. After that, Ian would head for the University, where his duties were flimsier than would be entertained now, in these days of 'accountability', 'external pacing', and other half-truths. However, Ian gave some stunning public lectures, and was fastidious in reading and commenting on student writing. He also organized a day of talks and readings in which Al Alvarez and Clive James participated, and he lined up a series of readings in the evening, which were a great success. There was one Wednesday where we absconded. Due to the Troubles, Northern Ireland were playing Spain at Hull City's ground, Boothferry Park. Both Hull City and Ireland were managed by Terry Neil, and George Best was playing. Faced with such a prospect then the only answer was 'Bugger poetry'.

On one memorable evening Philip Larkin joined us for dinner at my flat. Lesley enjoyed cooking for Larkin and prepared his favourites – crêpes fruits de mer, peppered steaks, bread pudding with sultanas, that sort of thing. What was said is now beyond recall, but the memorable bit was Ian's lack of appetite. It was more than conspicuous when confronted with bread pudding. Larkin ate Ian's as well as his own. Having ever been fond of my dinner, Ian's ascetic dining habits always seemed to me a perfect disgrace. I remember lunch in the late and lamented Bailey's Bistro on Greek Street where Ian started with an avocado, and ended with another avocado. God knows what was sopping up the contents of several carafes of House Red. Perhaps he'd enjoyed a large break-fast, though I doubt it. Later, I gathered that Ian's reluctance to eat stemmed from childhood experiences such as being forced to eat the fat off chops.

Having been a fan and follower of *The Review*, and frequenter of its Greek Street offices and The Pillars of Hercules practically next door, I was in on the launch of *The New Review*. Splendid as it was, it seemed ominously lavish. Others may well write more about *The New Review* in this book. It still strikes me as the best literary magazine we've ever had, while Hamilton's skills and acumen as an editor I believe to be almost radically wasted as a consequence of the disasters that afflicted that fine publication. Equally true, though, is that if the magazine had been a runaway success in terms of subscriptions and sales, then we may well have been denied such wonderful books as his biography of Robert Lowell, his witty if thwarted account of J D Salinger, his book about literary estates and posthumous fame, *Writers in Hollywood*, and now his admirable book on Matthew Arnold. When students come to me asking how to write an essay, I find myself promoting Ian as the finest prose stylist of our time. Invariably, they go away with a list of his books. When they come back, having read some of them, they agree with my opinion of his stature. There is such a coolness of tone, an even-handedness, a reasonableness of concern, that the effects are not those of detach-ment or diffidence, or of a distance between writer and subject. Instead, the result is the very opposite. His assertion of *style* comes across as being in itself Ian's measure of the seriousness of what he's writing about. It's almost as if he has to rise to the challenge of writing at least as well as the authors who form his subjects. I've known students on a course I teach on Modern American Poetry come to me from a reading of Ian's biography and tell me they think it's better than Lowell's poetry. Certainly, of all the critical or biographical works I've ever set as a professor, Ian's book on Lowell is one for which the students have expressed a real enthusiasm. Very often students express an eagerness for a poet's or a novelist's or a dramatist's work. To hear this said of a critic or biographer is much rarer.

Much as I esteem and value Ian as a critic, reviewer, essayist and biographer, it's his poetry which means most to me. More than any other poet alive he lives up to Larkin's conversational maxim, 'You can't write a poem unless you've a poem to write'. Ian rephrases the same conviction when he writes 'I suppose I thought that I would wait for poetry to happen rather than force myself to go in search of it'. Introducing his *Fifty Poems* in 1988, he wrote: 'Fifty poems in twenty-five years: not much to show for half a lifetime you might think'. Well ... yes; but the circumstances of poets are all very different. Some don't even need to crave 'the expansiveness and bulk' Ian refers to – it happens as part of the poem or poems they have to write. There's a rueful wisdom in Ian's preface to *Fifty Poems*. But it's *his* wisdom about his own writing of poetry. It discloses his cardinal virtue – an unwithering if also constantly anxious honesty. At times, though, it can seem like a reluctance to go over the page. To describe his poems, as Peter Porter does, as being like the masts of the scuttled German Fleet at Scapa Flow, as well as being witty, suggests the strength of Hamilton's poems. They're the tips of stories. But they're also melodic, uncannily so. Consider the haunting tunefulness of these lines:

> O world leave this alone
> At least

> This shocked and slightly aromatic fall of leaves
> She gathers now and presses to her mouth
> And swears on.

Or these:

> In the delicately shrouded eye
> Of this white rose, a patient eye,
> The eye of love,
> Knows who I am, and where I've been
> Tonight, and what I wish I'd done.

In his recent collection, *Steps*, although with just ten poems, the same half-whispered but distinct and audible cadencing can be heard. To write with simplicity about difficult and often painful subjects is one of the most important achievements to which a poet can aspire. Hamilton is like a present-tense Hardy without, of course, the versification and awesome productivity. Frost, Lowell and Larkin have all been among poets influential on Ian's work, and at times it shows. Unlike the first two, though, Ian seems determined to avoid the pigeon-holing of a 'poetry-pro', keeping his poetry separate from his other literary work. The presence there of Lowell and Larkin, as well as Frost, ought to remind us of the differences between the poetry scenes of the 1960s and 1970s. Those of us who were impressed by Larkin and Lowell can only feel puzzled and disappointed by the extent to which their reputations have been pushed to the side. Instead of the two Ls, the poetry world seems dominated by the School of Ashbery, the School of Muldoon, the School of Heaney, and so on. As the editor of *The Oxford Companion to Twentieth Century Poetry in English* may have to admit, the poetry-pros seemed to have gained the upper hand. At least, for the time being.

Ian Hamilton and I took flight to Australia in May 1987, in order to attend an international conference on literary journals, convened by Ian Donaldson and held at the National University in Canberra, a symposium and spree where Jeremy Treglown and Peter Porter would also be present. Ian and I were booked by mistake in different parts of the plane: I was Business Class to Ian's Economy, and I used to stand at the top of a staircase in our airborne Odeon and peer for him among the huddled masses at my feet, a scene from Dante. This, I told myself, only joking, must be what major writers feel when they look down on minor ones. We stopped for a night in Singapore. Rattling from the airport towards the city, I engaged the taxi-driver in liberal talk about its political situation – until I felt a gruffness coming from my friend, who was to prove a benign but caustic travelling companion. He unbent, however, at the Taj Mahal of an Indian-owned hotel, where free saunas were on offer. I turned on the television in my room. The political situation appeared to involve government-service, air-hostess, American-sleek Asian sylphs, reading the news. We went down in the lift, to claim our saunas.

I found myself sitting for an hour, stripped, wallet in hand, beside a steaming kettle in a wooden booth. My sauna over, I stepped into the corridor. There, at an open door, stood Ian, robed, steamed, smoking a cigarette, and flanked by smiling girls who were hanging on his few words. Could these be former readers of *The New Review*? Where were the readers of the *London Review*? I could hardly be looking at a love nest, I presumed, but this was a lot better than a kettle. Economy Class had taken its revenge, as Ian stood on the threshold in the posture of the iron man or transcendent lad extolled in the writings of Ruskin – in no wise evaporating, melting, maybe, but losing none of his weight.

We zoomed off over the endless forests of Java to Australia, where lads are larrikins and 'larrikin' is a literary critical term. It seemed as divided as the old *New Statesman*: a vast desert hinterland, vying with a suburban south-east coastal strip. Melbourne, where we arrived, seemed nineteenth-century at moments, with a ghostly after-sense of the Frontier, and with some nice merchants' houses about the same age as my own, an architectural feature over which Ian didn't want to hear me exclaiming. The scene was even further than I'd anticipated from urban Britain, let alone from the crowds and tumult of Bombay, which I'd yet to get to, up there at the opposite end of the ocean. India and Australia have distinguished newspaper and periodical traditions - well portrayed, respectively, in a film of Satyajit Ray's and in the writings of Sylvia Lawson – and Australia's current literary condition seemed hale and disputatious. We also seemed to have arrived in a country where the men and women did not go about together.

Canberra has been said by Barry Humphries to have become a little sleazy. He was joking, as so often. A garden city of civil servants, deserted after dark in its homogeneous recentness. An air of filing-cabinet propriety. Low-density housing lassoed by empty motorways and parked about a pastoral landscape of pastel colours, soft-smudged with eucalyptus, loud with the song of vehement birds with names like Major Mitchell's Cockatoo.

The conference was attended by agreeable people of several sorts – among them, the cosmopolitan Grazia Gunn, later to marry the convener, Ian Donaldson. The gathering concern with America which has been reported of Australia may have muted the country's traditional concern with the British literary culture, but, as the choice of speaker indicated on this occasion, it has not extinguished it. This was not an occasion, however, when a colonial deference was likely to be paraded. There were theorists in the audience who hailed from, but could hardly have approved of, the old country, and there were those in the audience who seemed to think that capitalist consumerism and English literature were finished, and that the true enemy lay on the moderate Left, among liberals, rather than in the conservative parties of the English-speaking world. And there were passages of arms when this conference on literary journalism seemed to have assembled in order to dance on its grave. I gave a lecture in which I boasted that the *London Review* was perhaps the only paper in Britain to oppose Thatcher's commitment to war over the Falklands, five years before. I sat down. Up rose a flaxen British Marxist feminist, domiciled in Australia, who asked why I had been so craven as to support the war. I was impressed by her not having listened. I had turned into the novelist and literary editor, Walter Allen, on a visit to Cambridge which I remember from the Fifties – an object of reflexive suspicion for the priggish young.

In July of that year Ian Hamilton digested, in the course of a Diary piece for the *London Review*, the lecture he'd given at the conference on 'Why little magazines don't matter any more'. The Diary dealt with his experience of editing his magazine *The Review*, and is a valuable account of what literary journalism can be like when purpose and pleasure coincide:

> For a brief period, I told them, *The Review* had most of the things I'd want a little magazine to have: it had a group of unknown poets it admired, it had a 'kind of poem' it wanted to promote, and it had powerfully-placed enemies it was eager to attack. It had youth, it had a sense of humour, and – looking back on it from now – a bumptious kind of certainty that it knew all the answers. It also had some sense of history, connecting itself back to an earlier epoch that was out of fashion: the poems it argued for had their roots in Imagism but would pride themselves on having far more human content than their models. And it had a sense of its own necessity. Pop poetry was coming into vogue and *The Review* was going to put a stop to that.

Karl Miller

In earlier days, said the Diary, the avant-gardists of the little magazines had been able to hold out against the mainstream for as much as a generation at a time. During his own editorial tenure, however, that had changed. Mainstream magazines, quality newspapers, formerly bored by or sour about avant-garde activity, began to take an interest in such journals and to draw their contributors away. *The Review* suffered accordingly, he felt; there were poets and critics who, under the duress of these solicitations, sank into self-parody. The seducing and suborning may still be going on, but it looks as if there are too few little magazines still around – too few good ones, at any rate – for it to be worth the big papers' while to keep an eye out. And I doubt whether the big papers are all that interested any more.

The papers I worked for were none of them little magazines. Ian's efforts were closer to the single-handed than mine were; I was never tied that closely to the one 'kind of poem', and I am not – nor is Ian – as avant-garde as the Diary might perhaps suggest. But I have no difficulty in responding to the hopes and aims described there. What he wanted to do editorially, he did. And he has done other things too, as various kinds of writer. All of these things seem to me admirable and lovable.

from Karl Miller's
Dark Horses (1998)

67

Alan Jenkins

Ian Hamilton had made a big impact on my life long before I met him or he knew I existed, but I can't talk about what I feel I owe him without getting personal. The nature of the man, and of what he has come to stand for, in my mind, would make anything else sound phoney or off the point.

I remember reading, aged fifteen, his poem 'The Storm' in the Penguin *The New Poetry*:

> You turn to me and when I call you come
> Over and kneel beside me, wanting me to take
> Your head between my hands as if it were
> A delicate bowl that the storm might break.

The address was so direct, so simple, and so delicate, the verse so unforced: this was poetry of the kind I could even see myself, one day, being able to write. And then, not long after, in an issue of the *TLS*, I saw 'Rose':

> But you have gone and so I'll call it wise;
> A patient breath, an eye, a rose
> That opens up too easily, and dies.

It's a perfect lost-love lyric, perhaps one of the finest lyrics by an English poet since the war (the others would be, for me, by Philip Larkin and Ian's friend John Fuller).

When he reprinted these and other poems from *The Visit*, along with some later pieces, just as perfect, like 'Larkinesque' and 'The Forties' in *Fifty Poems*, Ian added a preface in which he admits the decision he'd made to 'stop thinking like a poetry pro, to stop fretting about "range" and "output".... indeed, to keep the whole business of "my poetry" quite separate from the rest of my so-called literary life; a life of book reviews, biographies, anthologies and

68

magazines.' (Ian's inverted commas, especially in his poems, are some of the best I know.) It made perfect sense to me, and would even have done so long before, when I'd become familiar with the 'book reviews, biographies, anthologies and magazines', when the essays rounded up in *A Poetry Chronicle* had given me much of what I thought (or thought I thought) about modern poetry, and the legends attached to Ian's 'so-called literary life' had given me a hankering for a literary life of my own, so glamorous and un-cissy did he make it seem.

I was probably too young and callow to wonder what happens to the poet who lives that life. I do remember going up to London on some errand one day towards the end of my time at university and being drawn as if magnetised to the Greek Street offices of *The New Review*, climbing the stairs with thumping heart in the hope of catching a glimpse of the great man. I was, I think, going to ask him for a job. How could he refuse? I'd wow him with my take on Eliot and Mallarmé ... He wasn't there, of course. In a tiny office spilling boxes and papers and copies of the magazine, a bloke not much older than myself offered me, as consolation prize, a copy of James Fenton's *A Vacant Possession*. I carried it away as if it contained the pages of Genesis from the Gutenberg Bible.

By the time *Fifty Poems* came out, I *was* leading a literary life, of a kind. I was doing the same job on the *TLS* that Ian had done twenty years before, some of my colleagues had worked with him on *The New Review* and I'd even been involved with someone Ian had fallen for, back then. I suppose a Freudian would have a wonderful time with it, but from all that confused prehistory one of my best memories is of my first meeting with Ian: we were brought together by the woman in question, in a little Italian place in Soho, and I didn't want to kill the father, not at all, though a bit of me might still have wanted to be him.

I would go on feeling that, intermittently, through many of the boozy lunches and even boozier dinners that followed. Ian's speech is exact and funny and (very) laconic – even when he's talking about poetry or football. One evening he asked me if I'd been 'writing anything' – we both knew he meant poems – and I, confusing, for a moment, laconicism with the ironic knowingness which is the English defence against anything seeming to matter too much, said that I hadn't and added some crack that was meant to sound wittily self-deflating or dismissive. Ian pulled me up, hard. It was the closest I've seen him get to outrage: I'd sold myself short but, much worse, I'd sold poetry short, poetry, still for him the only activity (apart from football) that mattered enough to be taken seriously, that couldn't really be touched by the weariness and cynicism of its detractors or the clamourings of its supporters. He didn't want to see me go down either path, and though he wouldn't remember it, it was an important moment for me.

Ian called a few days ago. It was a coincidence; he had no idea, of course, that I'd undertaken to write these few words about him. The use of the telephone was in itself unusual. His preferred method of communication is by postcard, a few sentences in a microscopically tiny hand. But he'd lost my address, and he was calling to say that he'd seen a poem of mine, published in that morning's *Guardian*, and that he'd liked it; it was very moving, he said, and well-made. The poem was about clearing my mother's things out of her house in preparation for selling it and moving her into a home – a home that wasn't her home. In the event she'd died before she got there. I recalled a whole series of conversations I'd had with Ian on the subject of mothers, the gratitude I'd felt at being able to say what I needed to say, to someone who understood uncannily well and said some things along similar lines himself. Then I felt suddenly, massively cheered up. The past few months had been hard: my mother's death, the defection of another girlfriend, who wasn't just another girlfriend – and I'd been strenuously making things harder. Now here was a reminder of the other life I sometimes led, the life of words, and a reassurance that this life, at least, hadn't come apart in my hands. The real point was that it was Ian who had taken the trouble to remind me (though again, he wouldn't have known how much it meant), Ian who had found the poem moving and well-made. If those were things I had assumed, for as long as I could remember, that poems ought to be, the assumption had come, by precept and example, from Ian.

I was working in a bookshop in '62, still in my teens, and had established an ambitious autodidactic programme, of which systematic theft was a crucial part. I stole a copy of the first issue of *The Review* (but lost it several years later during one of many moves from slum to slum). I can remember now the sense of excitement at what I found: wit, irreverence, good writing, that conversation between Al Alvarez and Donald Davie ('I thought your piece was *moving* all right, but I wasn't sure in what direction...'), and, more than anything, the underlying notion that poetry was a serious business, that it should be taken seriously, that I was free to take myself seriously. I wanted to confront every ragged-trousered philistine, every smirking sophisticate, who had ever used the term 'your poetry'– *your* poetry – and roll the mag into a tight cylinder, and slap them silly with it.

Over the next few years, I sent *my* poetry out to magazines, had some limited successes, but also collected the apprentice's inevitable sheaf of rejection slips. I had a roster; a rota. Returns from the *NS* went straight to *The Observer*. *The Observer's* batch bounced back and went to *Encounter*. *Encounter's* SAE barely touched my doormat before it was on its way to *The London Mag*. I thought of the postman as a fickle bastard. Sometimes a sheaf sent back by *The Review* would be forwarded at once to the *TLS* and, as a straight swap, the *TLS* rejects would go to *The Review* by the same post. I didn't know that, with this exchange, manuscripts were regularly criss-crossing to the same man: Ian Hamilton. This must have gone on for a year or more, until I got a note from Ian to say that he was taking a poem for the *TLS*. He didn't mention the gormless duplications, but he did suggest we meet at Printing House Square.

I was jumpy about the meeting. London made me jumpy. People in the swim made me jumpy. I was living with a wife and two small children in a two-up, two-down hovel in the middle of a field, hadn't been to university ('Waste of bloody time. Get a job'– A E Harsent, *dec.*), didn't know which knife and fork to use and worried a lot about revolving doors and lifts. My response to Ian's invitation was to put on a tie. And a sports jacket. When I got to *The Times* building, Charis Ryder came down to tell me that Ian had had to go to the dentist. I didn't know, then, what a momentous piece of information this was. Cheesed-off, or else slightly relieved, I got the train back to Buckinghamshire.

I returned a week later and we went round to Dirty Dick's. I was determined to look good, but had no idea of what 'look good' might look like. I asked for a Scotch, which seemed right, though I rarely drank it, and told Ian that I had just been shortlisted for the Cheltenham Festival prize. He smiled that smile of his – just a tilt of the lips, skew-whiff, what I've come to think of as kindly-sardonic – and said that yes, he knew I had. Despite the smile, I still didn't get it.

I mentioned the doubled-up submissions. He just nodded and said something like, 'Yes; I've been watching your stuff for a while'. He told me that he thought I had strong affinities with Hart Crane, a poet he much admires. I said I couldn't see it, and immediately wanted to bite my lips off. The smile cropped up again. He said, 'No. Why should you?' and asked me if I'd like to publish a pamphlet with *The Review*. He also asked would I mind if he showed my poems to Jon Stallworthy at OUP. It was the beginning of the end of envelope stuffing. I was the English Hart Crane.

Later impressions of that meeting were of someone reserved, wary, softly spoken, wry – attributes I took for confidence and worldliness, but later came to view as enthusiasm tempered by caution. One of Ian's unfailing characteristics is loyalty to a cause; loyalty to a standpoint, really; a way of seeing the world. It extends to people, but that might take a little longer; there are good guys and bad guys.

I got the Cheltenham prize; Ian published the pamphlet; Stallworthy published the book. That was '69. I had found a job with a London publisher and was going home less and less often. London life involved seeing a lot more of Ian. I remember going down Greek Street for the first time, heading for The Pillars of Hercules, looking left and right at the porno stores, the strip joints, the peepshows, the hookers' calling cards. When Ian was setting up *The New Review*, and doing a deal for office rooms over a knocking shop, the landlord asked him why he wanted the property.

'I'm starting a magazine,' Ian said.

'Oh, yeah. Right.' The guy nodded. 'A magazine.'

'No, no, a literary magazine.'

'Sure.'

'Stories, poems, articles, stuff like that.'

'Sure'.

'Book reviews.'

'Sure.'

We would go to the Amalfi in Old Compton Street, where Ian would order the veal *al limone*, because it was the cheapest thing on the menu and, anyway, he wasn't going to eat it. Or else we went to a place round the corner that was pioneering the all-day breakfast. I'd already got Ian down as a kind of class-fellow, but all-day breakfasts clinched it. Everyone went in for Olympian drinking. It was like being in training. In training for drinking. No bottle was ever drained before another bottle had been ordered. Ian would start to look edgy at about two-thirds empty; well, a half to two-thirds.

The same thing with cigarettes. Sometimes he'd reach for his pack even though he had a cigarette on the go: just checking – eight in the pack? Six? That's tight. There was always a back-up pack, of course. But what if this *was* the back-up pack? That's *really* tight.

A life in restaurants … Martin Amis's mischievous theory that poets can't (or shouldn't) drive must, I suspect, have its origin in the fact that Ian has never been behind the wheel. By the same token, I'd bet long odds that he can't cook. Hasn't ever cooked. Is half-surprised to learn that things actually *have* to be cooked. Nothing I've seen of him leads me to believe that Ian has ever knocked up an amuse-gueule, though it's true he's sweated a vegetable from time to time.

There was a Greek place in Westbourne Grove; that was for evenings. I remember a meal there with Ted Hughes, who had just won, I think, the City of Venice award, and had been put up for it by Ronald Bottrell, who was also there, with his wife. I was intrigued to meet Bottrell for his odd elevation by Leavis: might there be something about the man that was (for sure) absent in the poems? Ian must have had something to do with the award, I suppose; maybe he was writing a piece; in any event, there was a whiff of duty about it all. He sized up the Bottrells and fell straight away into boredom. The boredom became edginess that could, as anyone who knows Ian would guess, easily develop into severe irritation. I was a pretty unruly sight in those days: long hair, beard, patched denim. I cringe to think of it. Mrs. Bottrell cringed, too, and remarked, unsmilingly, that I resembled a wild man. A look came into Ian's eye that heralded, I knew, a special kind of persistence.

'Does he? What do you mean?'

'The hair and so forth.'

'That's pretty insulting, isn't it?'

'No, I don't think so. I just –'

'You called my friend a wild man.'

'It's his appearance, not –'

'Maybe you could apologise.'

'I was just referring to –'

'Good idea to apologise.'

'All I meant –'

'I think you'd better apologise.'

As I remember it, Ted Hughes somehow got between them. It was all the more admirable of Ian since, earlier in the day, I'd revealed to him that I was a lifelong Chelsea supporter. I wish I'd been there the evening Ian had his fist-fight with John Berryman. Not so much for the slugging, but for the slow burn; the language; the step-by-step stuff: the *persistence*.

From what I remember of the people I knew at that time – the late Sixties and through the Seventies – it seems that debt and emotional chaos were written into the deal. If some of us had problems, though, with Ian it was a lifestyle. He woke up to it and bedded down with it. In the Pillars, once, I was bellyaching about life getting in the way of art; about being broke, about having to work. 'I just want it to be... you know... literature, *poetry*. Spend all my time on that.' Ian spread his arms like a man holding out the linings of his pockets. 'I have. Look at me.'

He was right; he'd given a lot, and he was still giving. That generosity provided one of the best literary magazine of the century; a magazine started (whatever anyone might think) out of passion and commitment and sustained by more of the same. There was a sense, however, that what Ian was best fitted for might be the life he already had. On one occasion, after I'd been hauled through a particularly bruising split-up, at bay in the Pillars, I said, 'That's all. Never again.' Ian said, 'You're a romantic; you'll come back for more.' He meant himself, too.

The New Review was a watershed in the lives of many young writers. Early work – sometimes first published work – by poets and novelists who are now established reputations; and work in each issue by writers who were, and remain, the best of their generation. The names are well known, and if you glance through back issues and look at the list of contributors, it's tough to see how even the colossal weight of envy and spite summoned up by the magazine's enemies could have managed to destroy it. Ian once said something like, 'A magazine like this needs its friends almost as much as it needs its enemies.' It's easy to see what he meant, and I don't think it was a matter of the friends being outnumbered. More a case, I reckon, of people in positions of power who simply didn't know, or care, how good the magazine was.

Ian knew who the enemies were: we all did. They were bad writers; or, worse, bad writers with influence. There was a policy, for sure, of being unsparing in reviews of second-raters and phonies; there was an equally strong policy of praising what seemed the best of its time. Standards were high and properly unyielding, which led to charges of 'elitism', a word as grotesquely misused then as now. Elitism and cliques. This was from people who would never be published in the magazine. The fact is that *The New Review* was a club anyone could join. Anyone good enough. Naturally, this was an attitude that required critical back-up, and the magazine obliged with a stringent and clear critical line. Ian once remarked of a poem that had been submitted, 'It's a piece of writing all right; might even be a good piece of writing; but it's not a poem.' I'd never quite looked at things that way before, but once I'd heard it, it sounded obvious. It's a test that ought always to be applied.

The critical over-view was almost as much a matter of who read the magazine as who wrote for it. I won't get this right because I can't find the source; but, in interview somewhere, Ian was asked what was the magazine's subscription figure. He said, 'About two thousand.' The interviewer asked, 'Wouldn't you like it to be more? Four thousand, say?' Ian replied, 'Maybe. But I'd need to know who the other two thousand people were.'

≈

I was reading an article about ageing yesterday, which said we don't have to do it. At least, not so fast; not so relentlessly.

It's not just wear and tear, it seems, but also a fault in the cells: after a while, they stop making new cells. Now, scientists are working on the business of preventing DNA damage. That way, we could live forever. Well, not us; it's already too late. And not forever; but maybe a thousand years.

The piece put me in mind of lines of Ian's that I quoted back to him once, because they seemed to me to have such a sting about them: 'You want to live forever/And I don't...' There's a whole novel in those lines.

> At one time we wanted nothing more
> Than to wake up in each other's arms
> Old enemy,
> You want to live forever
> And I don't
> Was the last pact we made
> On our last afternoon together.

It's called 'Friends', and the sad irony in the title is almost unbearable. Like others of Ian's poems, it identifies at once a certain emotional climate, what we like to call 'voice'. Commentators have said of it that it's bleak, or wry, or withdrawn, which might be useful and true, but it strikes me most forcibly as a uniquely lyrical, passionate, and sorrowing voice. There's no one better at describing a world by inference; his diction and cadences draw you in immediately. There's no one better able to express the almost-said, or to make careful, incisive and ironical use of gesture and moment. He has a method for isolating the quotidian and transforming it: in his version, the brutal quotidian; the inescapable; the embattled; and sometimes, surprisingly, the hopeful-against-the-odds.

Lines

for Ian Hamilton

Two blackbirds were pretending to speak Swedish
at four in the morning, as I lay awake
putting the finishing touches to a work
of homage: musical, minimalist, unmodish . . . .

No, I wasn't. I was wrenching words
for rhymes – these same, poor, clapped-out hack words –
while out in the garden two never-repetitive blackbirds
were doing their free-jazz thing with the other birds.

Girls Girls Girls Ian Hamilton (centre) outside
The New Review Offices 11 Greek St Soho c. 1974

Ian McEwan

I don't remember what led up to my moving to London in January 1974 from my cheap, comfortable flat in Norwich. I took an attic room among the roofs and TV aerials of Stockwell, in a house belonging to an antiquarian bookseller called Cyclops. He had left school in his mid teens and gone to live in Paris, in the Beat Hotel during its one brief moment. There he developed a romantic passion for literature the like of which I haven't come across in anyone else since. He had an eye patch and tough guy good looks and was able to bring home a series of impossibly beautiful women. One of them, a West Indian girl from Brixton, moved in with us. She and I sometimes overlapped in the tiny kitchen where I would be preparing my lunch while she thought about her breakfast. All afternoon she would bathe, make up and dress, in preparation for Cy's return from his shop on the King's Road. Then the good time would begin, and the house would throb until dawn.

Part ex-hippy, part country mouse, I moved warily about this household. I thought I had left this kind of high life behind me in Kabul two years before. I was serious, I was here to write. I had cut my hair well clear of my shoulders and had grown a scholarly beard. Cape was bringing out a collection of my stories, but not for another eighteen months. Up in my attic I began work on more stories, but I soon began to wilt in the discovery that every writer never stops making – writing is not enough. And it's difficult to do in isolation. Where was the city, the life, I had discarded Norwich for? My one literary contact was Jonathan Raban who had given up his teaching job at the University of East Anglia and gone freelance. He lived in Earls Court, in the basement flat of a house belonging to Caroline Blackwood and Robert Lowell. Here I learned about a new magazine rising out of the ashes of *The Review* and was advised to call on the editor.

I've never bought the myth of Ian Hamilton as literature's flinty enforcer, the man of 'eyelids thin with scorn' who slashed your copy to tatters and waited there contemptuously while you fixed it. True, even back then he had the face of a capo di capi, and a useful, understated cool, but I came to think of him as a kindly sort. We sat in his office at 11 Greek Street and I explained what I was up to. His manner was pleasant, even avuncular. He took the story I had brought and suggested we went downstairs for a drink. The Pillars of Hercules was *The New Review*'s outer office and unofficial club room. It was midday and there was no one else around. We stood at the bar drinking large gin and tonics – a novelty to me then – and Ian asked me questions about my family background. I suppose I could, or should, invent a riotous story about our first meeting but the memory of it blurs into the next dozen occasions. The bar behind us fills with writers, many of them poets I had never heard of, and the long office party of the mid-Seventies begins.

In The Pillars I met 'my generation' of writers – male, born in the late forties – and made friendships that will last me a lifetime – among them Amis, Barnes, Raine, Fenton, Reid. Most of us had yet to publish our first books. We read each other with close, gossipy attention. It was a given that there was nowhere as good to place a story or poem as *The New Review* – at least, until the Amis-Barnes era began at *The Statesman*. If this was a literary clique, it was remarkably open. I took various friends along who weren't really writers at all, but Ian treated them as though they were and gave them books to review. Anyone, it seemed, could wander in and get a drink. Junkies came in to shoot up in the lavatories upstairs. If you wandered in too often, you were likely to be given an unpaid job. Mine was at a desk in a corner of the packing room on the second floor. Ian asked me to read the short story slush pile and tell him if there was anything worth his consideration. It took me two weeks to discover that there wasn't. We tinkered with the idea of publishing a selection of the covering letters whose emotional range had impressed me. Later, I helped with distributing the magazine and learned where all the bookshops in London were. There were surprisingly few in those days.

Because of the hospitality in The Pillars, *The New Review* attracted unfriendly coverage in the press. The magazine was said to be too expensive, too glossy, too obscene sometimes and generally too self-confident for a publication humbly dependent on public funds. Above all, it stood accused of being an excuse for a piss-up. There was a grain, a dram, of truth in this, but the writing and editing got done, and to the highest standards. Ian was the sort of editor writers wanted to please. He didn't hand out praise, or even condemnation; it was silence, neither lofty nor benign, more a kind of butch restraint, that worked the trick. I was never told that the story I had brought along that first time had been accepted. The fact trickled out somehow and I sensed that it was correct to hide one's delight. I was made aware that if I presented another story, there was a chance it might get read. There was no method to this minimal touch – it was simply a consequence of Ian's character. A few years later I worked with Richard Eyre and found that he unconsciously worked a similar trick; he stood back at rehearsals, open to whatever might come up, and the actors worked intensely to appease the reticence that awed them.

Back in my Stockwell attic room, I worked more happily as the months passed. I had somewhere to take my fiction, I had contemporaries to talk to and read. The trips to Greek Street gave me a short story, 'Pornography'. Sometime in early 1975 I had a long conversation at the bar with Ian about the difficulties writers face with their second books. Out of this came a story, 'Reflections of a Kept Ape.' Excited by the new poetry I was reading, I handed in a poem about a man who was turned into a dog by a vengeful woman. Considerate as ever, Ian lost it. He started an occasional series in which writers reminisced about family life – writers and their families have been a running concern in his own work. I promised to contribute, but after a week I was stuck. When I complained that I was finding it difficult to write the truth about my family he said curtly, 'Make it up'. This was how I began my first novel, *The Cement Garden.*

The story goes that none of the contributors to *The New Review* was ever paid. This wasn't quite true. I was paid for almost every story Ian published. You had to show persistence, and you stood a better chance with him if you didn't have a regular job. I remember going into The Pillars once with Seamus Heaney, whom I had just met. We found Ian at the bar, bought him a drink and got him into a dark corner – we didn't want the sight of his chequebook starting a general stampede. I came away with thirty pounds and Seamus with ten. Over lunch at the Chinese fish and chip shop in Berwick Street, elated by my success, I offered the poet expansive advice on raising his earnings. When I met him again, a year later in California, he kindly pretended to have forgotten the incident.

The younger writers who hung around *The New Review* came of age in the Sixties. Ian, however, was a child of the Fifties. In the hot summer of 1976 a dozen of us were eating supper at pavement tables outside a Greek place on Charlotte Street. This was at the time of a reckless fashion among certain writers for smoking cannabis in restaurants. A smouldering parsnip-shaped concoction came Ian's way and he stared at it with contempt.

'What's this?'

'You smoke it.'

He took three or four long drags, then screwed the rest into his ashtray. 'You're meant to pass it on,' someone protested.

'But you gave it to me.'

We watched him closely for signs of transformation. He took a slug of his drink, picked up his cigarette and went on talking. Not a flicker. Very cool. We were impressed.

This was an exciting time for me, so it would be easy to sentimentalise *The New Review*. I had no involvement with the running of the magazine, but it was clear to everyone in the Pillars that Ian was under pressure. There were debt collectors, problems with distribution and circulation, a hostile press, the Arts Council threatening to pull the plug – which it finally did. There was also some heartache in the private life, as well as domestic problems that sometimes required Ian to go chasing across central London in the small hours for the protection of someone close to him. He didn't complain. In fact, he didn't talk about it much and you got the feeling he didn't want to be questioned. But it wasn't always possible to conceal the strain – on one occasion his hair turned white overnight and started to fall out. Within a week or two it was black again and starting to grow.

Apart from the occasional double issue and a sudden shrinking of format for the final two issues, the back numbers of *The New Review* retain nothing of this turmoil. In fact they've stood up well against almost a quarter of a century. Turning the pages now, what's apparent is a rare combination of cultural openness and fierce literary standards. Another triumph of *The New Review* was entirely transient, and not one that history is likely to thank the editor for; however, Ian's achievement has some bearing on the question of how we support writing in this country. What he managed, probably without meaning to, was to create a milieu. Writers gathered around *The New Review*, as they had around *The Review*, because they respected Ian's ideas of quality, and they felt flattered to be included. I doubt if there has been a period in English literary history when so many writers have filed through one pub. Writers read each other, obviously; they are bound to deny it, but they write for each other too, in a remote and buried sense. This is particularly true for those at the beginning of their careers. We might prefer to portray ourselves as lonely beacons in a dark world, but when our first stories or poems are printed it means a lot to know that a few contemporaries we admire are reading them.

When I am asked how – or whether – writing should be subsidised, I always say this: what writers, particularly young writers, need is a classy magazine with a charismatic editor; it should be culturally eclectic and have exacting literary standards. It should be metropolitan, because most writers and readers live in cities, and its editorial offices should be near, or above, a pub. The contributors should be decently paid. Ian probably looks at his complete set of back issues with mixed feelings and memories – those were turbulent days, not always happy, but the writing got done. When I look at my old *New Reviews*, however, I tend to think that this was one of the wisest pennies the literature panel ever spent.

Craig Raine

The Buried Life: Two Recovered Memories

1. 'A cough shouldn't stop you smoking. You just need a bottle of Benylin.' We were in The Pillars of Hercules, the pub more or less next door to the offices of *The New Review* at 11 Greek Street. I wasn't smoking. I had a cough.

'What's Benylin?'

The Bogart persona intensified. The operational side of Ian's mouth spoke: 'What's *Benylin*? Benylin's the first drink of the day.'

I was Books Editor. The magazine was only just surviving. Ian's thick hair had started to fall out in handfuls. Pure stress. We never mentioned it.

He rented a flat in Dean Street, over the Japanese Steak House. Maybe I would like to use it some time, rather than get the milk train back to Oxford? He didn't need it. All I had to do was ask for the keys.

The one time I stayed there, Paul Theroux's *The Consul's File* was on the bedside table. Otherwise the place gave nothing away. It was as unadorned and functional as a budget hotel room anywhere. In the kitchenette, the handles on the cupboards and drawers were black bakelite crescents. Not a single one was intact.

Before I got into bed I arranged my padded jacket over the pillow. In case it was ringworm, not stress after all.

At 4 a.m. I was woken by a machine outside breaking bottles for half an hour. I went to the kitchen for a glass of water. Irritably going to open a cupboard with my middle finger, I understood how the handles came to be snapped in two. Thirst. The first drink of the day.

The magazine folded. His hair recovered. Ian recovered.

2. We were in The Pillars of Hercules. Ian was at the bar, his back to me, buying the drinks. Just as he was turning, I asked, 'How was your weekend with Matthew?' (His nine-year-old son by his first marriage.)

He could hardly speak. His eyes were spangled with tears. 'Great.' My own eyes filled. Then we recovered.

And that was exactly how the poems were supposed to work. The laconic lifting into lyric. Tight-lipped. Vulnerable. Irresistible.

Dan Jacobson

Chronic Block?

So far as they can be said to be famous at all, Ian Hamilton's poems are famous for being small in size and few in number. In a recent issue of *Poetry Review* (Autumn/Winter 97/98), Ian Sansom took out a slide-rule and figured that he has averaged 'less than two poems a year ... Each poem no longer than about twenty lines, with about ten words to a line which makes ... about eight words a week.'

So what is he up to? Why doesn't he pull himself together? What kind of model is this to present to the ambitious, productive, word-processing generations following his own? In the Introduction to his *Fifty Poems*, published by Faber in 1988, Hamilton speaks almost apologetically (for him) on the subject. He admits that 'in certain moods' he used to crave 'expansiveness and bulk' and did consciously try to incorporate into his verse 'more narrative, more satire, more intelligence, and so on'. But he soon learned that it wouldn't do. Not for him; not as a poet anyway. Whatever liberties he might permit himself to take in prose, the poems he actually wrote came to him, he says, 'out of the blue'. Exacted from him by painful circumstance, they were 'spoken in a voice... made musical by a kind of anguished incredulity, a refusal to believe that fathers die, that wives go mad, that love... is not enough'. Elsewhere (in an interview published in the issue of *Poetry Review* quoted above) he says that his poems were 'based on the old idea of inspiration, on the "miraculous" notion that you are visited by the poem. If a poem is not there, you will never find it, no matter how hard you look...' Describing this notion as 'infantile' or 'Romantic', he nevertheless remains loyal to it.

About his repugnance to the idea of narrative in poetry he remains unrepentant. In a letter to the *Times LiterarySupplement* (April 3, 98), he writes that he is 'still not keen on narrative poems', but generously allows that he would not want to see them 'forcibly suppressed', as he might have done in 'the good old days'. In the *Poetry Review* interview he is more expansive on the subject, but scarcely any more forgiving:

> The Imagist project was quite important to me... [Ezra Pound] had a problem with poems with a lot of unnecessary furniture. He felt that the poet should get to the heart of the matter, to the maximum point of intensity, and then get rid of the furniture. You don't need 'And then he walked across the room and opened the door and slapped her in the face'. You want the slap. That's the poetic bit. The other stuff is the narrative leadup; it might as well be in a novel. One of the difficulties is that the walking across the room and the opening of the door have to be implied. You must give a sense of setting, past events, likely future events.

There we have it, then. The poem as slap. The slap as poem. Everything else left out. A 'sense of setting, past events, likely future events' reluctantly thrown in solely for the slap's sake. It is about as austere, even self-mortifying, an aesthetic as one can imagine. As a reader of the poems, however, I have a problem with it. Or rather, two overlapping problems. First, I have never been able to think of his poems as anything but narratives: truncated, cryptic narratives, narratives sometimes so urgently bent on denying their own inner drift as to appear positively maimed by the effort; but narratives nevertheless. Secondly, and more generally, a slap which we see given by one unknown person to another – in the street, say, or even in the corner of a room at a party – is likely to do not much more for us than to leave us feeling vaguely stirred, embarrassed, curious; at best ignorantly sympathetic to one or other of those involved. But this?

Dan Jacobson

Now and Then

The white walls of the Institution
Overlook a strip of thriving meadowland.
On clear days, we can walk there
And look back upon your 'second home'
From the green shelter
Of this wild, top-heavy tree.

It all seems so long ago. This afternoon
A gentle sun
Smiles on the tidy avenues, the lawns,
The miniature allotments,
On the barred windows of the brand-new
Chronic block, 'our pride and joy'.
At the main gate
Pale visitors are hurrying from cars.

It all seems so far away. This afternoon
The smoke from our abandoned cigarettes
Climbs in a single column to the sky.
A gentle sun
Smiles on the dark, afflicted heads
Of young men who have come to nothing.

Admittedly, I have chosen here one of the more explicit and extended of the poems to be found in the Faber collection; it is also – no doubt for that reason – one of the poems in the volume that I admire most. But it resembles many others in the fragile steadfastness of its tone: in its capacity to combine intimacy with aloofness, yearning with sarcasm, sharp observation with a gaze that is seemingly averted from what matters most to the speaker. However frugally we may be fed with novelistic 'plot' or motive, it

91

is impossible for us to feel that the two chief figures in the poem are strangers merely, no more than people glimpsed from the top of a bus or through a half-open door. We have been compelled to enter their lives, just as they have been set free to enter ours. To a lesser but significant degree the same applies to the others who appear in the poem: those pale, hurrying visitors, the young men 'who have come to nothing', even the unidentified speaker of the phrases in quotation marks. We know what they are about; how afflicted they are by their own or others' afflictions, and the shifts they adopt in trying to deal with them.

How is it done? Through the words of course – what else? – placed exactly in this syntactic order, punctuated in this fashion, disposed on the page to make these visual and musical patterns and to suggest one particular tale. Through the inseparability, too, of each of these elements of the poem from all the others. Notice, for example, the unexplained or unassigned pronouns (which recur over and over again in Hamilton's verse): in this case the central 'we', the possessive 'your', the first 'our' which is put within inverted commas even before we get to it. It is for us to pick up each pronominal referent: a task which in some of the author's more bleakly gnomic poems is made difficult, even baffling, but which here actually helps us to come closer to the speaker than we otherwise could. His voice is like that of a man speaking to himself; he knows who the *dramatis personae* are and why they are placed in the circumstances in which we find them; paradoxically, therefore, for him to supply them with proper names, or to identify and externalise them in any other manner, would merely distance us from both him and them.

A comparable effect is achieved by the deliberate disarray of the tenses in which or through which or beyond which (so to speak) the 'action' takes place. Everything in the poem is given to us as if it is happening now, in the present, as the words are uttered – 'This afternoon'. (The phrase is twice repeated, along with 'A gentle sun'.) But in that case how are we to take the poem's title, 'Now and Then'? Are we to assume that things now are different from what they were in the past? During past visits? Or in the past that existed before such visits were necessary? Or are we to read the title in its more casual, everyday sense: i.e. every so often? (Hamilton's ear is always attentive to the possibilities hidden in turns of speech which the rest of us take for granted.) And what, amid this bewilderment of times and occasions, is the status of 'It all seems so long ago' and 'It all seems so far away'? Long ago from when? Far away from what?

Well, I suppose we have all had the experience of standing in one place and yet feeling ourselves to be elsewhere; of living through emotions which we cannot repudiate but which diminish rather than strengthen our sense of ourselves. We also know what it is like to find ourselves subsequently puzzling over the strange combination of intensity and disconnectedness which marks such moments. No wonder, then, that the carefully weighted re-animation of yet another common colloquialism which concludes the poem should generate so much power. To 'come to nothing' is to arrive at as forlorn an end as can be imagined; an end which is rendered no less final by its appalling indefiniteness. (The men in question are still 'young', after all.) Notice too how the image of their 'dark afflicted heads' has been prefigured psychologically and metrically in the 'wild, top-heavy tree' which appears in the first stanza. What might initially have looked like no more than a merely decorative item, a bit of scene-setting, is thus transformed into an integral part of the poem. Much the same could be said about the smoke from the couple's abandoned cigarettes climbing 'in a single column to the sky'. What could be more closely intertwined and yet more insubstantial than this embrace?

Many of the poems in the Faber collection end in assertions much more directly threatening than the last line of 'Now and Then'. 'The storm rolls through me as your mouth opens' ('The

Storm'). 'And wait for an attack' ('Birthday Poem'). 'It's perfect night in you. And then you scream' ('The Recruits'). 'Your final breath/Is in the air, pure white, and moving fast' ('Midwinter'). 'If I had touched you then/One of us might have survived' ('Epitaph'). 'In ten seconds we will hear it break' ('Anniversary'). 'You won't remember this' ('Remember This'). And so forth. In each case the poem breaks off just before the moment of rupture or crisis towards which it has apparently been heading from the start. This abrupt thwarting of our narrative expectations, the speaker's inability or refusal to 'normalise' what is to follow by giving his account of it, becomes the very point of the poem: an act of abstemiousness or self-abnegation which helps to convey a sense of irremediable loss. Oddly enough, however, it can also strike one as a positively dictatorial expression of will. Silenced by pain, the poet silences all the other presences in his poems, whoever they may be – lovers, friends, his father, earlier selves, even himself assuming the role of poet. (See the poem grimly entitled 'Poet', the sixth and final line of which reads simply, 'Folly...'). The reader is turned away. Only the particulars evoked by way of startlingly active metaphors (the headlights of trucks that *slop* into a room; a train *simmering* under a station roof; yellowed drifts of snow *cleansed* by a moment's fall; a friend left *chewing* unhappily on his whisky; cars on a dual carriageway *cool, expectant, happily pursued*; a tree *afloat* outside a window; a coffin that *skates* 'into the fiery deep') are allowed to survive. So are the emotions fused with them. The rest is blank. White paper.

Call me a softie if you like – or a democrat – or a novelist – but my own inclinations draw me towards those poems which end in a less assertive and more open fashion; not so much in silence, as it were, as in reflection or doubt. In fact, in Hamilton's latest pamphlet (*Steps*, Cargo Press, 1997), half the poems do literally begin or end either with a question or a series of questions. Among them are several of the most affecting he has ever written. 'We live in dreams' he wrote in an earlier poem; in these, however, he has managed to incorporate some of the puzzlement and necessary inconclusiveness of dream-states, without ever losing control of the work or diminishing the freight of experience and desire he has always wanted his lines to carry. 'What we see today,' he says severely in *Poetry Review* 'is more what poetry *is not* than what it *is* .... Every line doesn't count, every word hasn't been carefully chosen, it doesn't have any structure, there's no reason why this line is broken and that line is not...You call *this* poetry? I think it's something, but I don't think it's poetry.' Compare his reprobations here with a poem from the new collection – one among several I would gladly have chosen.

Again

>That dream again: you stop me at the door
>And take my arm, but grievingly.
>Behind you, in the parlour, I can see
>The bow of a deep sofa, blanketed in grey,
>And next to it, as if at harbourside,
>A darker grey, rough-sculpted group of three.
>Three profiles sombrely inclined,
>Long overcoats unbuttoned, hats in hand:
>Night-mariners, with eyes of stone,
>And yet the eyes seem stricken.
>Is it that they too can hardly bear
>What's happened. What *has* happened? Who?

That writing of this order does indeed deserve to be called poetry; that it is utterly distinctive to him; that he has never allowed himself to be deflected from it by the storms of his life, or the expectations of others, or the demands of his career as an editor, critic, and biographer – for all this, and much else besides, I will always be grateful.

Over the last thirty years, during the dark days as well as the lighter ones, Ian has always found time to read and to comment on my plays. It is not only out of gratitude for this, but for many other and perhaps even more valuable reasons, that I intend to dedicate this play to Ian. He knew it in one of its early drafts as *Cornered*. Its title, when it is finally ready for full publication,† will be, I think, *Just The Three Of Us*. What follows is the first half of the play's first scene.

Simon Gray
27th April 1998

ACT ONE

Scene One

Late evening.

A cottage studio, with an open–plan kitchen and bathroom off. A bed on stage, a table, two chairs, one armchair, French windows opening on to balcony. Shelves crammed with books (Dickens, Tolstoy, etc.), a cassette player and various tapes and compact discs of classical music.

Hanging from the ceiling, stretching down from the highest point in a corner, is a considerable length of chain which goes through a pulley and vanishes as if leading up to the roof. The chain is not particularly noticeable. The door of the studio is open. There is a bottle of Scotch on the table. Also a bottle of dandelion wine.

ENID   is standing at the French windows. She has a glass of scotch in her hand.

RONNIE   is walking up and down studio, agitatedly, puffing at his pipe, glass of wine in his hand.

† Note: It finally is, and will be published by Nick Hern Books in February 1999.

ENID: (coming in) Now, what were you saying Ronnie? Oh, yes, something about your church roof, I expect, whenever I can't remember what you've been talking about it's always the church roof, people being rained on during your sermons, plaster falling into their hair – is that it?

RONNIE: No, my dear, I wasn't talking about the church roof. I was asking you if you're sure her name is Toni Gray, it seems to me it hasn't been Toni Gray until now.

ENID: Nonsense, Ronnie, she's always been Toni Gray, of course she has. (Takes a long drink) For as long as I've known her.

RONNIE: But, my dear, you've never even met her. You've only talked to her once. On the telephone.

ENID: But I know her. Through and through. Indeed I do.

RONNIE: Well, be that as it may, I still don't think she's Toni Gray. Nearly but not quite. She's got a chap's name, yes, beginning with a 'T', yes – and a colour – yes, a colour – the note! Did you remember to put out the note?

ENID: Note? What note?

RONNIE: The note telling her to come down here and not to the Big House.

ENID: Yes, yes, of course I did, I must have done, I remember quite distinctly making a note to myself to put a note on the front – you're flustering me with all these questions, Ronnie, why are you flustering me? Why do we have to talk about it? I don't want to think about it even. It'll happen as it happens, when it happens, whatever arrangements I've made or forgotten to make, and that's all we need to know. (Makes to pour herself another large drink)

RONNIE: My dear! Um, would you like a glass of dandelion, Mrs Price's dandelion instead – (picking up bottle)

ENID: Oh, don't be ridiculous, Ronnie! (Pouring whisky)

RONNIE: But – but do you really think that that's wise?

ENID: Of course it's not wise. Wise doesn't come into it.

RONNIE: But if you're going to do this, if you're really going to do this, my dear, you're going to need a clear head.

ENID: No, I don't. I don't. A clear heart, a clear will, that's all I need.

RONNIE: Very well, my dear. (Watches ENID taking another gulp of whisky, then looks at his watch) She'll be here any minute, I'd better get going. I'll look in – I'll look in in an hour or so. As – as planned. All right, my dear, and – and good luck or – or –

ENID: Yes, yes, in an hour. No, earlier. Half an hour! Come in *half* an hour!

RONNIE: Half an hour. Right, my dear. (Moving to door)

ENID: No, no, don't go at all. Stay here, Ronnie, I may need you.

RONNIE: My dear, we agreed that this bit has to be entirely private. I can't possibly watch, I mean, I'm a vicar after all –

ENID: Well then, well then – don't watch, go in there! (Indicating door)

RONNIE: What – in the lavatory! Hide in the lavatory! Really, Enid! No, no, I can't – I can't.

ENID: Ronnie, if you want me to go through with this –

RONNIE: My dear, I don't want you to go through with anything you don't want to go through with. That's been my position. Right from the very start.

ENID: Well then, if Fred wants me to go through with it –

RONNIE: Fred's position would probably be exactly the same as my position – that is, if he had any idea of what it is you're thinking of going through with. But as he doesn't, he can't be blamed for not having the position he would have if – if – he knew um –

ENID: So you're blaming *me*! Is that it? Blaming me, on top of everything else. Hah!

RONNIE: No, no, of course I'm not, Enid my dear, we're not talking about blame, blame doesn't come into it –

ENID: 'Oh, Enid, Enid, I'm sinking into the marsh,' he said. 'Going straight down the tubes, into the marsh. Save me, Enid, my dearest and last hope, as always.' And he was crying when he said that, Ronnie, yes, I could see tears trembling down his cheeks. And you, Ronnie, you went down on your knees in that way you always do when you're shocked and moved – 'Oh, save him, save him yet again, Enid, I beg you. Only you can do it!' Isn't that true, Ronnie? Isn't that what you said, and what he said?

RONNIE: Well – not quite as I remember it, my dear. Certainly not in those words anyway. 'Down the tubes' possibly, because that's his usual phrase when he has a crisis – and perhaps something about a marsh, yes, I remember being struck by the marsh, not having heard it before, but as for tears and crying – no, no, I think he was his quiet matter-of-fact self, and as for me, I may have gone down on my knees but that was merely to add a little weight, there was no question of begging for him, not at all – and besides, we weren't talking about what you're thinking of doing now, we would never have dreamt of asking you to do this, good heavens, I mean a criminal act! No, no, this has nothing to do with what we were talking about, we were talking about, well, the hope that you'd return to your trusty typewriter and give Fred a new Lady –

ENID lets out a scream, puts her hands to her ears.

RONNIE: Sorry, my dear, sorry. I didn't mean to mention – I was just trying to explain – that there's no connection, really, between the one thing and the other.

ENID: There is a connection, indeed there is! If I'm going to be deprived of my calm, my happiness, my health itself, then Fred's going to be deprived of something too, that's only fair! And that's all I ask. Tit for Tat. His tit for my tat. (Lets out a yap of laughter) And if you're going to deny me, Ronnie, then we can just go back to where we were. Me, to my peace and good health and he to his – his tit, as he goes down the tubes into his marsh, yes, I'll really not begrudge it to him, not at all, so you 'phone him, Ronnie, go and 'phone him –

RONNIE: My dear, my dear, please – if all this is simply about my going into the lavatory, why then – why then, of course I'll go into it.

ENID: Thank you, Ronnie. (Calmly, then emotionally) You're a dear, dear man, Ronnie, I don't know what we'd do without you.

RONNIE: Thank you, my dear. I don't have to tell you how much, how very much you and Fred –

Sound of car approaching.

RONNIE: Oh, there she is! But that's – that's Fred's car!

ENID: Fred! What do you mean! He hasn't come too!

RONNIE: No, no, my dear, what are we thinking of, it can't be him – impossible. Well, I'd better – (hurrying towards lavatory) I just hope she doesn't want to use it – (goes into lavatory)

ENID: (tries to take up a dignified position, stumbles slightly) Oh – oh, dear.

As sound of car door slamming, footsteps on gravel.

ENID rushes to sink, splashes water on to her face, then unable to help herself, runs to bottle, turns away from door and gulps down scotch, as:

TERRI enters, briskly. She is in her mid-twenties, carrying handbag-briefcase. Sees ENID with her back to her.

TERRI: Mrs Parkhurst?

ENID: (puts glass down, turns) Yes, can I help you? Oh, you're my husband's PG, aren't you?

TERRI: Well, his PA, Personal Assistant.

ENID: Oh, of course. PA. Not PG, PG used to be a paying guest, and we don't have those any more, do we? But the name's Gray, isn't it? Toni Gray. Ms Toni Gray, as we have to say these days.

TERRI: Green actually, Mrs Parkhurst. Terri Green.

ENID: Ms Green, I'm so sorry. And Terri, you say. Well, we knew it was a 'T' and a colour, didn't we – (as if to RONNIE) Anyway, you saw my note, that's the main thing.

TERRI: Note? What note?

ENID: Didn't I put a note on the door of the house – the Big House – saying that I'd be down here in the studio and not up there in the Big House? I'm sure I put it up because I made a note –

TERRI: Well, I didn't see any note – I didn't stop at the house, you see, because when we talked on the telephone you told me to go past it, around the bend to your studio. Actually, you said that I couldn't miss it because if I did I'd be over the cliffs onto the rocks and I'd be dead.

ENID: Oh, we wouldn't want that, would we, you down there, dead on the rocks.

They laugh together.

TERRI: But what a lovely place.

ENID: It was the bottom part of an old lighthouse, you know, I come down at all hours of the day and night, when I want to get away from the Big House and mull things over, mull them over all by myself, it's my mulling place. Mulling place. Do you have one of those?

TERRI: No – no. I wish I did.

ENID: What a nice answer. And I'm sure you will. Yes, I'm sure you will. (Smiles at TERRI) Well, anyway, here you are, safe and sound, for this – this surprise business. This birthday surprise. For my husband. He's looking forward to it enormously. No, no, what am I saying, how can he be looking forward to it if I'm going to surprise him with it? Where is he at the moment, by the way, my husband?

TERRI: He's – he's in Frankfurt.

ENID: Oh yes, Frankfurt. Of course he is. Why?

TERRI: Well, he's gone to the book fair.

ENID: Is that it? – yes, I find it so difficult to follow his comings and goings at the moment. Sometimes he seems to be all over the place all at once. But why are we standing? What about a drink? Let's sit, shall we – and (pouring herself one) There's this or (seeing wine) Ronnie's daffodil (shudders)

TERRI: Oh, no, I'd better not, thank you. Driving, you see.

ENID: Oh yes, of course you are, we heard the car, didn't we? (As if to RONNIE) I mean I did, I heard the car. Did it take ages?

TERRI: An hour and a half about. To hit the middle of Dover.

ENID: An hour and a half! To hit the middle - hit the middle of poor old Dover! You must have driven like a demon, my dear. What sort of car is it?

TERRI: A Porsche.

ENID: A Porsche, I don't know about cars but it rings a bell. A Porsche – is it blue and very expensive, like Fred's?

TERRI: Well, it is his, actually.

ENID: Oh, I see, you've got my husband's car then, have you?

TERRI: Well, it's the company car, actually. So we're allowed to use it when – Mr Parkhurst's away.

ENID: Well, I never let him use it down here, except at week-ends when he usually comes down, not his company car nor any other kind of car. Absolutely forbidden. We're bicycling folk down here, go everywhere by bicycle. Or on foot. Except when we take the train. To go to London – and such places. And how do you get around normally, my dear, when you haven't got my husband's company car? What methods do you use?

TERRI: Well, I live out in Harlow so I've been taking the train to Victoria and then the tube to Sloane Square and then a bus to World's End. And there I am. Apart from a bit of a walk. But there may be simpler – methods, I've only just moved there.

ENID: What, my dear?

TERRI: I've only just moved there. Harlow.

ENID: Harlow? Moved to Harlow? Why would you do that, my dear?

TERRI: Well, I don't know, really, come to think of it. It must be the nomad in me, or something - but just when I'm really settling down somewhere and making a proper little home for myself, then I'm up and off to somewhere else starting all over again – I mean apart from Harlow now, I've lived in Willesdon, Neasdon, Ruislip, Finchley –

ENID: Hamburg, did you say?

TERRI: Hamburg? Oh, Freddie – your husband, I mean. No, Frankfurt. For the book fair.

ENID: And he doesn't take you with him? To such a seedy, sad and lonely place, Frankfurt? Doesn't he need you there?

TERRI: No, no, he needs to have me in the office. Especially when he's away.

ENID: Needs to have you in the office especially when he's away. Must be difficult for him. (Lets out a hysterical yap)

TERRI: Pardon?

ENID: What, my dear?

TERRI: I thought you said something.

ENID: Oh, no. It was a yap. I do that sometimes, yap. What do you make of the moustache?

TERRI: The moustache?

ENID: Yes, the moustache. His. Fred's. His moustache. What do you make of it?

TERRI: Um, well – I – I haven't really thought about it. (Laughs) But it's very – very – well, it seems to suit him.

ENID: Suit him, yes, yes, that's the secret of it, isn't it, that it just belongs there. Well, it could hardly belong anywhere else, could it, being a moustache. (Laughs) He grew a beard once, you know, black and ginger, thick, black and ginger stubble is what it was really, made him look like something out of Macbeth, especially when he was drunk. Oh, how you must adore working for him, Fred, and his moustache. Tell me, what are your precise duties, my dear, as his personal – or are they all merely personal, too personal to talk about? (Laughs)

TERRI: No, no, not at all. Well, I do some editorial things as well, quite a few recently, I mean recently he's asked me to look at manuscripts oh, not the highbrow ones the philosophy, the religions and the – the (gestures) I'm useless for those, don't understand a word of them – but the romantic fiction. What Freddie – (checks herself) Mr Parkhurst calls the bread and butter *and* the jam.

ENID: Oh! bread, butter, jam. Yes. That's what romance is to Fred, bless him, butter, jam, that's all it is, is that what it's to you too, jam, butter, bread?

TERRI: Well, well, I absolutely love reading it myself. I mean – I mean I'm a sort of addict. The perfect reader, Mr Parkhurst says. If someone like me likes it, it'll make a million. I remember the first I ever read, it was when I'd just started working, it was by Lizzie Heartbourne, one of her Lady Goforth's –

ENID lets out a scream, puts her hands over her ears.

TERRI: Mrs Parkhurst?

ENID: (checks herself, laughs) Oh, I'm sorry, my dear, it was just that I knew you were going to say that somehow, I just knew it.

TERRI: Yes, well, she's so famous and brilliant, isn't she, I've read everything she's ever written, some of them again and again – 'Love is a Dragon', 'Oh, Heart, Oh, Heart, Oh Hunting Heart' – and her Lady Caroline Goforth series 'Go Forth with Courage', 'Go Forth with Hope', 'Go Forth with Honour' – I wish she'd write another one soon, I miss her. So does Mr Parkhurst. He says we – well, his company, what it desperately needs right now is a new Goforth from Lizzie Heartbourne so he can stop worrying about not being able to pay for all his really important books. So you love her too, do you then, Lizzie Heartbourne?

ENID: Oh well, she may have a talent for telling stories, I suppose, but they're still tosh. Soppy tosh, that's what they are, soppy, soppy, tosh, tosh. (Viciously) I'm so glad she's stopped. A drunken mess of a woman, Heartbourne, revolting. But then look at me! Enid Parkhurst. Also revolting. Quite revolting. But then we're all revolting, aren't we, my dear?

TERRI: (After an embarrassed pause) Well, as for the party, the surprise party for – your husband – I've made out a sort of provisional guest list. (Hands list to ENID) And of course we have to discuss the – um – the venue.

ENID: (Takes list, stares at it, unfocused) The what?

TERRI: Well, where you want to have it.

ENID: Have what? (Studying list)

TERRI: Your surprise party. For your husband's birthday, I mean.

ENID: What's this, I can't make it out, all these names –

TERRI: Well, they're everyone from the office and the agents, and some of the sales people – along with all Freddie's – Mr Parkhurst's writers.

ENID: But *she's* here, Lizzie Heartbourne! (Glaring at TERRI) I've just told you how much I hate her and despise her (strikes name off list) We want real people, real friends. The people Fred grew up with, the people who love him. Like me. Like me. His Enid. I'll be there, you know.

TERRI: Well, of course you will. But (awkwardly) I don't know any of the people from Freddie's private life. You see.

ENID: Nor do I. Not any more. (Begins to cry)

There is a pause.

TERRI: (desperately) Perhaps the best thing would be for me to go away and leave you to – to think about it and – and I'll give you a ring before – um – your husband comes back from Ham – Frankfurt, so you can think about his past –

ENID: I don't want to think – I don't want to think about Fred's past. That's the last thing I want to think about. His past. Thinking about his presence is bad enough. What? What do I mean? Present, I mean. He's not present – his absence I must mean. Yes. I – I – (stops, stares helplessly at TERRI) My dear?

TERRI: (gets up) Well – it's been very nice to meet you, I'll be in touch before – before – he comes back. (Goes to door)

ENID: Yes, yes, go away, good-bye – oh, no, no, one thing I need you to help me with – come back – come back just – just for a second, it'll only take a second –

TERRI comes back.

ENID: Stand there. (Rocking slightly on her feet) Now here, let me take this – (takes handbag from TERRI, puts it down. TERRI stands, concealing impatience) Now, it's this, you see – (lurching around her, picks up chain) this. You – you – how does it go, Ronnie? Oh yes, you put it around your waist – your tummy – will you do that for me – really, only a second.

RONNIE opens bathroom door slightly, peers out, unseen by TERRI, as TERRI puts chain around her waist.

ENID: Yes – a little tighter, I think, eh, Ronnie? Ah, that's it, perfect. Now, you see – (Takes out of her pocket padlock, hands it to TERRI) if you just put this through this – and this –

TERRI clicks padlock around her waist, stands there, patient but bewildered.

ENID: (steps away, claps her hands) Done it, done it! Didn't think I could do it, did you, my dear? there, look at her! I've got her!

RONNIE closes the door quietly.

ENID sits down, stares gloatingly at TERRI. TERRI stares back, bewildered. She attempts a little laugh.

TERRI: Well, um –

ENID: How does it feel? I mean, what are you feeling?

Reminiscences of Several Kinds

Ian was embedded in my usually unshiftable and always poorly evidenced demonology when I first met him. I recall that this was at a party given by Alan Brownjohn while he was living in Chelsea or thereabouts in the Sixties. Both Alan and Anthony Thwaite had told me what a remarkable person Ian was, and how much they liked and admired him. I was stuck in the rut of The Group Poets of whom he was a severe castigator. So when I was introduced to him I tried to glower, and I remember mounting some sort of argument that to demolish most of the verse you encounter is not the best approach to criticism. I probably referred to that scene in *Candide* where Martin and Candide are shown over his library by Senator Pococurante. The Senator dismisses all the greats – Homer on to Milton. When they leave, Candide remarks to Martin that here surely is a great man as he is superior to every admired book in his library. Martin responds that the strongest stomachs are not those which refuse all food. I've used this example dozens of times since, and I suppose I still believe it. But whatever was said on that occasion, I came away convinced that I had misunderstood Ian – certainly that his belief in poetry was the most absolute part of his character. I was equally sure that he expects from poetry more than I could ever look to find in it. For me there must be piles of chaff as well as grains of wheat, otherwise we may be conned into taking high-rise chaff for real wheat. Also, we must leave it to posterity to make the final grading however convinced we are of our immediate valuations.

That meeting with Ian, however, was the beginning of a connection which has been intense but sporadic. As it developed I came to appreciate him as a general judge of literature, as a great humorist, a wonderful editor and an unequalled distinguisher of fine prose.

At this time, the middle of the Sixties, Ian and Gisela were living up the road from me in Paddington, in a flat in Westbourne Terrace. Emerging from the side of Paddington Station, I would sometimes be hailed by Ian from his balcony as I walked down Chilworth Street, and we would find ourselves in one of London's least attractive pubs. This was called something like The Railway Terminus Hotel: today it has been updated by the corporate designers to join the catalogue of phoney hostelries in the Firkin Chain, The Fettler and Firkin. Its sheer lack of glamour and paucity of comfort made it the right suburban extension of The Pillars of Hercules in Greek Street, which mise-en-scène doubtless will be recalled by many contributors to this book. I remember talking about poetry in that pub much more than in the Pillars. There is a sort of urgency given to one's seriousness by the sense of dereliction of duty, of trespass even. You have to press home a topic when you know that the cauliflower is going dry and the meat carbonising at home. It was then also that my first wife Jannice and Gisela got to know each other.

Jannice, far more than I, was witness and helper in Gisela's troubles. This is a private matter which I should not discuss in print, but it led to an aspect of Ian for which I am grateful. Jannice's death in 1974 was, with few elements of doubt, a suicide. But there was the inquest to be endured. There were special circumstances surrounding her death, but even more there was the certainty that respectability in her home town, Marlow, wanted an open verdict. I wasn't sure what I would be called upon to say, or whether I would have to give evidence. Anyone who has been in this position will know that, even had his conduct been more wholly admirable than mine, he would not be certain that he could justify himself. The inquest was being held in Slough. Ian insisted on accompanying me: without his support I doubt I could have gone through with it. I have always been uncertain about the relationship between real events and literature. This will sound naïve – perhaps what I mean is that writers can be admirable realists on paper and cowards in life. Observing Ian showed me what the pressure behind his poems amounted to. For him the flurry of so much poetry was indulgence, or at best a swamping of feeling by adipose detail and opinion. We either desire to embellish each crisis with social comment, and history and pattern-making, or we face up to it in verse as directly as in life. For Ian the words which frame a crisis must be so evocative that they can dispense with unnecessary evidence or justification. A Hamilton poem, at least at its ideal, must accelerate from stand-still to climax in a few words. This had struck me only negatively when I began to read Ian's poetry in the Sixties. Adapting some of Martials's *Epigrams*, I dedicated my version of Book 8 No. 29 to I.H.

> The short poem signals
> much suffering suppressed –
> like the German Fleet at Scapa Flow,
> only the flying pennants show!
>
> Such terseness shames all us
> chapter-and-versifiers –
> but what's the point, since Fabers took
> enough to make another book?

In 1974, after Jannice's death, I understood what the Hamilton poetry method was for, though I could not follow it. I wished, as I still do, that the width of Ian's erudition, wit and scurrility were given scope in his verse. There are signs that this is happening in his recent book, *Steps* (Cargo Press, 1997). In 'Resolve' the personality of the interior monitor is, for all its more relaxed manner, the same 'Thin Controller' of the early Hamiltonian poetry. But here is a more sardonic attitude towards the poet's desire to make a truthful poem.

> Enchantress, know-all, Queen of Number, Muse,
> You knew all this. And what do you know now?
> None of the same you'll say,
> But toothless, blind, forgetful. Well, perhaps.

> Unlock my hands,
> Let's call this 'for the last time'.
> When you go,
> Don't murmur, as you used to, 'Yes, I know.'

There is always a problem when the poet refuses to be a 'chapter-and-versifier' about who is meant by the second person pronoun. As the passage quoted seems to suggest, imagination becomes androgynous, or maybe it's just that Conscience is essentially female. What grows on the reader of Hamilton's verse as the years pass, is the conviction that all his poems are etchings and not, as prejudice once suggested, smudges.

The impressive canon of *The New Review* will stand in vindication of the Pillars of Hercules days, but when I think of those times I am drawn to Clive James' *Peregrine Prykke's Pilgrimage Through The London Literary World*. Book Three of this golden epic paints a picture of days at The Pillars which no novelist could improve on. Ian's apotheosis as Hammerhead – how many readers, I wonder, shared Clive's and my recognition that a hammerhead is a fearsome but actually gentle shark common on the Australian coast? – is yoked with Klaus Mauler's (Karl Miller's) and Terry Towelling's (Kilmartin's) as Perry Prykke's introduction to the galley-slave world of book reviewing. Facing the beginning of Book Three in the 1976 edition is Russell Davies' illustration of the interior of The Pillars in which Ian is centre-stage, mugs and glasses arrayed waiter-wise along his arm, with a willowy Hugo Williams and a diminutive Douglas Dunn behind. All Davies' caricatures are as accurate as Beerbohm's, but his of Ian which I enjoy most is not in *Perry Prykke* but adorns a late issue of *The Review* in which contributors were asked to consider the state of literature at that time. Davies draws Ian as a Prince of Denmark kicking a football round the ramparts of Elsinore Castle. It's interesting to reflect how many of today's admired, even legendary, reviewers got their start from Ian in more or less the way Prykke does, though usually with fewer barbs addressed to their self-regard. Ian is also Falstaff-like in being the occasion of wit in others. *The Complete Works of Edward Pygge* can justly be deemed Hamiltonian though the majority are not by Ian's hand. *Prykke* also owes its existence to Ian. In its ur-version it was the set-piece at *The Review's* cabaret for *Poetry International, 1974.* The previous year had witnessed the *Pygge Manifestazione* at the ICA where Bob Lull brought his *Notebook* emendations to their triumphant apotheosis. Ian might think it not much of a compliment but I consider him the Cyril Connolly of our age. In my book, this is great praise.

≈

A few vignettes to end with.

I am standing on the corner of Bayswater Road and Gloucester Terrace just by the Lancaster Hotel with Ian. We are looking for a taxi. I propose a competition. Let's see who has the pulling-power to conjure a taxi: it is nearly rush hour and none seems to be about. I wave, gesture, move into the road, but all the taxis are occupied or those which seem empty ignore me. It's then Ian's turn. He raises his hand and three unoccupied taxis appear at his side. Much the same happens in bars. Perhaps it would too if he were feeding the ducks or scattering crumbs to goldfish.

~

It is 1977 and Ian has arranged a memorial reading for Robert Lowell at the Anglican Church in Redcliffe Square. Celebrities of all sorts waft in. I have never since sat within touching distance of both Isaiah Berlin and Mary McCarthy. Seamus Heaney gives the address. But what makes the occasion memorable is Ian's decision not to use recorded music but to call on his brother-in-law to arrange a live recital. It is strangely moving to listen to Richard Lewis with male chorus and piano accompaniment (not organ!) indulging in the throbbing lyricism of Edgardo's 'O bell'alma inamorata' from the last scene of Donizetti's *Lucia di Lammermoor*. I had always imagined Lowell to be tone deaf, but this wild lamentation must have wafted up to him in some patrician Bostonian Heaven.

~

Ian is at the Gazebo Hotel in Sydney's King's Cross and refuses to go out as he intends to watch the Cup Final, which reaches Australia at an unsocial hour. Back on my home soil I appreciate that I will never be an Englishman. Empson appends, as epigraph to his poem 'Part of Mandevil's Travels', King Abdullah's remark at the Woolwich Arsenal when invited to fire off a new torpedo, 'I feel half an Englishman already'. No exposure to the terraces would make an Englishman of me. Listening to London literary people talking football, I have exchanged looks with Clive James. Why is football so important? But perhaps Gazza is the price we have to pay for such brilliant books as the biography of Lowell and *Keepers of the Flame*.

When you get onto the big wheel of writing (or the little wheels within wheels of poetry), it seems clear to me that the people you look to and feel an affinity for are not – to begin with, anyway – the ones who get on immediately before and after you, still less the ones who've been on for ages – you want their seats – but the half-strangers you see through the struts half a cycle (half a generation) away, falling as you rise, rising as you fall. There were three poets I had my eye on – probably all appalled to be mentioned in each other's company, and by me: Joseph Brodsky, Tom Paulin and, most intimately though I knew him least, Ian Hamilton. When I sent him a copy of my first book, I realised I'd even purloined his initials for my title.

I wasn't of an age to have been reading, never mind submitting to, his magazines, *The Review* and *The New Review*, but when I started publishing around 1980, I had his book of poems *The Visit* (1970) on permanent loan from the English Faculty Library at Cambridge. It would fall due and I would renew it. I must have read it quite literally hundreds of times – and everyone else not at all! 'No one shaved, and only the turtle washed,' as Lowell said of the turtle in the bathtub. I discovered Hamilton, I suppose, and should explain, in the place of honour at the end of A Alvarez's *The New Poetry*, second edition. When the time finally came for me to leave the rocky bosom of Cambridge, I was in a dilemma over the book. I couldn't live without it. Finally I said I'd lost it, paid the ten pound penalty, and thought I'd got away with murder: no doubt George Washington would have behaved differently. Now I'm the proud owner of four or five copies (whenever I come across one, I buy it), and moreover Faber had the grace to publish an enlarged version in 1988, *Fifty Poems*, so the library will be back in business too. Greetings, borrowers.

Michael Hofmann

What I admire – not the word – about the poems is their intensity. John Berryman once said: write as short as you can, in order, of what matters. Surely no one – least of all Berryman himself – can have fulfilled the terms of that prescription as scrupulously as Hamilton. The majority of the poems are generated by one of two subjects: a wife's mental illness and a father's death from cancer. The few exceptions, just as sombre, are barely to be distinguished. There is something terrible and heroic in this narrow focus, in the way that these few poems, produced over so many years, should have settled so close by one another, with their themes of break-up and break-down, their shattered atmosphere, their identical reference points of hands and heads and flowers and grass and snow and shadow. That 'silence on other subjects' that Brecht mentioned in a quite different context is part of the effect. Nothing else, Hamilton implies, can have any being next to such losses. Each individual poem is pruned back to an austere and beautiful knot of pain. Poetry, by his practice of it, is not craftsmanship or profession, but catastrophe. I can't, in general terms, think of any better way for a poem to be. Most poems have a hard time answering the question: 'Is this really necessary?' Not his.

Fifty poems on fifty-one pages – there is one, 'Larkinesque', that goes 'over the page'. Exactly half of them ten lines or fewer. A verbal account of an image of an experience: a double distillation, a world away from the stuff that deserves the nasty label 'confessional'. A bit of 1910, a bit of 1960, and a bit of 1860 in the stately Matthew Arnoldesque crumble of the iambs. They are physical, without losing themselves in materialist drift; scenic without being pretty; verbally effective but not finical or clever for the sake of it. Thought wrestles with feeling, word with thing, and the poem balances. The 'I – you' stuff reminds me now of Montale; the beauty and compression and sorrow of Chinese poetry. The title poem 'The Visit':

They've let me walk with you
As far as the high wall. The placid smiles
Of our new friends, the old incurables,
Pursue us lovingly.

Their boyish, suntanned heads,
Their ancient arms
Outstretched, belong to you.

Although your head still burns
Your hands remember me.

There is an echo of Yeats (impossible to hear 'ancient' without it), quite a bit of 'Waking in the Blue' in the humorous commingling of health and sickness, but the thing doesn't seem literary at all: the tenderness and delicacy and terror of the last two lines are original and primal.

One wishes, reflexively, there were more; but then again, why should there be, or what would there be? Hamilton talks about it in his pained and nobly frank preface to *Fifty Poems*: 'Fifty poems in twenty-five years: not much to show for half a lifetime, you might think. And, in certain moods, I would agree. In certain moods, I used to crave expansiveness and bulk, and early on I had several shots at getting "more of the world" into my verse: more narrative, more satire, more intelligence, and so on.' More, in other words, would not, could not, be more of the same, and what then would be the point, beyond allowing the poet to think as he puts it, 'like a poetry pro'? One realises one has been thinking like a reading pro, and feels – not that Hamilton would have intended that – rebuked.

Stood alongside *Fifty Poems,* most things just look impossibly trite, leisurely and overstuffed. When Hamilton was judging the *New Statesman's* Prudence Farmer Competition some time in the Eighties, I remember he commented on how many of the poems had food in them. My own poems go like sequences of television quiz show prizes, undesirable prizes, prizes for losers, just one darn thing after another! Even with his example before me, how materialistic I have become, even in my own brand of negative materialism! How crass and compendious! *Fifty Poems* contains nothing in the way of comestibles: cigarettes, 'J and B' and 'a haze of cultivated blossom'. Pick your own! No, I'm wrong: the last poem on the last page, 'The Forties', ends:

>   the neat plot
> For your (why not?) 'organic greens',
> The trellis that needs fixing, that I'll fix.

Well, it hardly reads like the Pauline conversion.

By grace of *anno domini* or whatever, Ian Hamilton is for me first and last a poet. If I'd been only slightly older, I would have been aware of the literary arbiter and infighter, the Sixties *Wunderkind,* the builder and demolisher of reputations, the Ian Hammerhead of his friend Clive James's skit on literary London. And if any younger, he would be the author of the books he's published since, that nebulous thing, a jobbing biographer and writer, almost in the American sense of the word, a magazine feature writer, a non-fictionist, a prose pro. The poetry-centred view of Ian Hamilton does two things: it sees something, in Hamilton's own words on Aldous Huxley, 'sad and impressive' about the subsequent prose career; and it organises the biographies and reviews, gives them a theme, a 'subtext' even, that otherwise they might not have. Still, always underlying everything is the callow, unexamined assumption that if a man has published a book of poems, he would prefer to publish more books of poems than anything else; and that if he could nominate fifty half-filled pages of his writing (all right then, fifty-one) that would endure, it would be his poems. Poetry pro that I hardly am, I feel that, and I guess Ian Hamilton does too.

John Fuller

A Breath of Fresh Air

I first met Ian in 1959, during my final year as an under-graduate. What a strange year that was! I was not to realise it fully at the time, but it was the year of Lowell's *Life Studies*, the greatest influence on Ian's view of poetry and a significant historical water-shed in many ways. In the parochial world of student poetry things were different. In the aftermath of the visit of Allen Ginsberg and Gregory Corso in the previous year, a disastrous wave of drugged and lower-case formlessness had afflicted Oxford poets fascinated by the Beat Generation's typescripts (drawn tantalisingly one by one from Ginsberg's travelling basket at readings). Already the university seemed to be tiring of the intellectualisms first introduced by MacBeth and Thwaite and somewhat perpetuated by Lonsdale and Spink. The work of my friends Dom Moraes and Peter Levi had a decidedly neo-romantic flavour. At the time, as a recent semi-surrealist, I had been fascinated myself by the 'great eye sounds' of Corso, and even quite proud to print his work along with that of Ginsberg, Kerouac and Burroughs (probably for the first time in this country) in *Isis*. But the general trend (soon to be reflected in the wilder productions of Cape Goliard or Trigram) wasn't at all to my taste.

For that reason, Ian's magazine *Tomorrow*, launched in the summer of 1959 with lashings of Michael Horovitz and thin jests from the 21-year-old Roger McGough, certainly passed me by at first. As a poet I wasn't much interested in the idea of 'tomorrow', and as a student facing finals I was too compulsively caught up in the past.

It wasn't until I encountered Ian in person, and experienced his demanding, dismissive, uncompromising sensibility at first hand that I realised that he didn't much like what he had been printing either. But a hungry man must eat something, and he was simply setting up his shop, and the shop-front was provided, impressively, by Oscar Mellor's absolutely authentic Fantasy Press.

120

John Fuller

I very soon arrived at a complete awe for the blue-chip value of Ian's commitment to little magazines. *Tomorrow* did matter, after all, and a poetry magazine wasn't just the glamour of history, Pound as procurer of modernism, etc, etc. It was a social instrument, a personal crusade. And poetry was, yes, as important as football.

Ian was different from most Oxford poets: tough, austere, unprivileged, unpretentious. He possessed a natural tight-lipped authority that paid no dues to the established channels of influence. I liked him immediately, and felt a strange surge of relief and literary homecoming of some kind when he took me on board. He induced me to review Donald Davie's *The Forests of Lithuania* for *Tomorrow* no. 3, and allowed my friend Francis Hope to do a hatchet job on Geoffrey Hill's first book. I think we both wanted to please, wanted to claim a place in a forum for which Ian's charisma seemed to guarantee a future. No matter that it was such a mixed bag. It would get better, we knew. And it did. The vastly expanded no. 4 contained, among other goodies, the first printing of Pinter's *A Slight Ache*. I knew that I had found a significant ally whose ambitions cast into the shade my earlier editorial flirtations (*Isis*; *Gemini*; *Oxford Poetry*; *Universities Poetry* – all in various ways circumscribed by local circumstances or the deadness of committees and their alien assumptions). I carried the poetry magazine virus in my blood, but I had never let it rage untreated. Ian was seriously infected, and I admired his single-minded genius.

But Ian was almost as unsatisfied with *Tomorrow* as he was with the magazine he had edited at school in Darlington (the contents of the latter ostentatiously consisting, as he ruefully confessed, of irritated letters from famous writers refusing to contribute). He had managed to ditch his co-editor on *Tomorrow*, but in the face of the financial difficulties which were for ever afterwards to haunt his editorial chair he wanted a new start. Valuable boxes of back-numbers were abandoned in a porter's store-room in Keble College because Ian, with a large battels bill unpaid, dared not risk being seen claiming them.

As we discussed possibilities during 1961 it became clear to me that Ian was a compulsive serial editor. It was rather like his smoking.

As our evenings wore on, Ian would become paler and more terse, his disagreements bleaker, his enthusiasms less vocal, his face drained – until he simply had to leave (wherever he was, whatever the hour) to find a cigarette machine. Without a magazine, he similarly became edgy, anxious, unfulfilled. The only relief was fiercely competitive bar-billiards, or darts, accompanied by the yeasty cloudy bottled Worthington that we liked to drink.

After marriage and graduation in 1960 I had to concentrate on my research, more exams, and eventually the negotiation of a job in the US. But I eked out my grant with reviewing, and could therefore commiserate with Ian who endured the constant slavery and distraction of WEA classes to keep the wolf from the door. Reviewing is flattering to the reviewer, who will feel that an important part of life is not merely writing poetry, but telling other people, whether they like it or not, how it should be written. It is, of course, really a way of learning the same thing oneself. This is why little magazines should only be edited by the young.

I was keen to be involved with Ian's new plans (which in August 1961 were for a magazine to be called, rather severely, *Evidence in Writing*), but I didn't much get on with his friend Michael Fried, just as I suspected that Ian didn't get on with Francis Hope, then at All Souls. When I aired all this, it was clear that Ian felt that antagonisms might actually be constructive, since we would be (as he wrote in a letter to me) 'a group that will generate ideas'. That we (and Colin Falck, the other major mover) didn't actually much meet at all didn't seem to matter. 'If the magazine is the place where these differences can be thrashed out', Ian wrote, 'so much the better'. He made it sound more like a football field than a forum of cultural devotion. Excellent! This instinct of Ian's was right. His management of any of his magazines' taste and direction was always more generously catholic than you might at first have supposed. There was in his experienced view no certain source of material yearning for print. He knew that the presence of a magazine would be enough to help him to find new poets and critics: 'We'll have to attract them,' he wrote. 'We'll have to create a situation in which they can confidently emerge from their caves and take a deep breath of fresh air.'

Thus in a short time (certainly by December 1961) it merely became a matter of what this new bi-monthly magazine was to be called and where the money was coming from. From my Bodleian desk, working on the early 18th century, Defoe's *The Review* sounded a retrievable title. It was severe enough, in one sense, but also relaxed and neither starry-eyed like *Tomorrow* nor forensic-academic like *Evidence in Writing*. It was going to be responsible and investigative, and also open-minded. The open-mindedness was always a little surprising to me, who knew very well the range of Ian's scorn. I never understood why, for example, he printed my long light poem in tetrameter couplets, ' The Art of Love' ('I loathe leisured, "witty", knowing poetry,' he had told me. 'I loathe that which is assured because it has so little to be in doubt about, I don't much care for *light*, satiric verse'), but I suppose it was for more or less the same reason as he went ahead later with an issue of Black Mountain poets ('I half agree with all you say about the Black Mt. people...but I think that in terms of information the number is a useful one'). The fresh air, therefore, was the sort that you get from your *own* mountain, ie. a view of everything else.

My influence on *The Review* was slight, and often disastrous. For example, the Gill Sans of the first three issues was entirely due to my illusion that we were somehow a reincarnation of Geoffrey Grigson. After that, the professional touch of Tony Russell put things right, and the authentic format was achieved. Many of the poets I contacted were devastatingly declined by Ian ('I have read the Moraes and think that if we were to print any of these we would be disarming ourselves on too many critical fronts' – I was tremendously impressed by such a prophylactic touch; it made me feel like a wittering amateur). When Ian finally found the poets who seemed to be exactly tuned to his critical frequency, the complete character of *The Review* was evident to everyone. (And incidentally, the superb recent work of Hugo Williams and David Harsent is alone justification of the magazine's ten-year existence.)

Those early years, with a fair amount of the magazine written by ourselves under pseudonyms and every subscription worth the celebratory drink which made a large hole in it, with darts or football (Beechcroft Road version) and with evenings of smoke-clouded conspiracy, were years for me never to be matched for excitement and sense of collective intent. Ian and I have both had other lives since, but our exchanges at that time were a critical benchmark of sorts for me, part of growing up. There are not many people who will tell you when your work 'won't do' and I am grateful to Ian for never disguising that truth. How easy it might have been to have lived within a world of ingratiation and false esteem! I am sure that all Ian's friends will agree that we who have been lucky to have known him have escaped such a fate. We have seen our dud manuscripts on his knee, whether in actuality or imagination, and we have been better for it (I refer to his poem 'Critique'). Even now, whenever I encounter some literary fatuity, especially one committed by myself, I feel the better for remembering his laugh of disbelieving wonder: the shoulders resigned, the brows raised, the mouth under severe control, the eyes narrowed and dancing, the cough, the air around him full of smoke. Race you to the sea, Ian!

A Lost Weekend In Malta

I first met Ian more than thirty years ago. I had been, for some time, a regular (and, in those days, anonymous) reviewer for *The Times Literary Supplement*. When the editor, Alan Pryce-Jones, left, I was kept on by his successor, a smooth old journalist named Arthur Crook, but I found it pleasanter to deal with his assistant, the much more agreeable Ian, and in due course we became good friends.

When I was appointed Literature Director of the Arts Council of Great Britain in 1971, I helped to persuade the Council to encourage into existence a new monthly literary magazine of national stature. At first, we attempted to land a distinguished middle-aged figure as editor. I remember trying to tempt Karl Miller into taking on the job, but he refused, and instead recommended Ian Hamilton very highly. *The New Review* began its life in April, 1974. Ian was a brilliant editor, and those fifty issues of the magazine stand as a remarkable achievement. It folded after four and a half years, mainly because of the envy of a number of people in the literary world (some of them members of the Arts Council's Literature Advisory Panel) who had not been invited to contribute to its pages. I seemed to have to fight for the magazine both inside and outside the Arts Council. Finally and inevitably, I lost the battle.

An agreeable piece of light relief from the rigours of Arts Council life was provided in 1974 when the Maltese Ministry of Education and Culture contacted me. They were setting up an annual European prize, the Malta Cultural Award, to be competed for by most European countries. The prize would be given for a book of literary essays published within the previous twelve months. Would I nominate the British entry?

I thought for a few moments. Who wrote essays any longer? Ah yes, Ian Hamilton had published a book of literary essays the previous year. As far as I could remember, no one else had. I nominated Ian. Some weeks later, I was informed that Great Britain, i.e. Ian, was the winner of the Malta Cultural Award. He and I were invited to Valletta, air fares and all expenses paid, for a weekend in May as the guests of the Maltese government. We flew out on a Friday, were met at the airport in Valletta and driven to our hotel. On Friday evening there was to be an official dinner given by the Minister of Industry, Trade, Agriculture and Tourism. Ian and I decided to skip this, and explore Valletta instead. We felt that honour would be sufficiently upheld by our presence the following morning at the prize-giving ceremony in the Palace of the Grand Masters.

Valletta is a dump. We ate a mediocre meal at an Italian restaurant in a sleazy street called, I think, The Cut, and then, since there was nothing else to do in the town, we began a tour of the bars. At some point in the evening, I seem to remember, we separated, no doubt in order not to cramp Ian's style. But we later ran into each other again in an otherwise deserted bar whither Ian's taxi driver had taken him as being the most likely scene of action.

Ian was later to recall that we intended to leave that bar together, having called for a taxi to take us back to our hotel. But he sauntered into the loo on our way out, and emerged just in time to see the taxi disappearing, with me in it. Next morning, I remembered nothing of this.

The next thing I did remember was being shaken awake by Ian. I looked around me. I was in our hotel, but in a room that was neither mine nor his. My clothes were strewn about on the floor. 'Thank Christ you've awakened me,' I said to Ian, 'or I'd have slept through, and missed the prize-giving. Hold on. I'll have a quick shower.'

'Have a slow shower,' Ian replied in his inimitably laconic manner. 'It's afternoon. I had to go to the ceremony without you.

I told them you were ill. Here's what they gave me.' And he waved in my face a cheque (for several hundred pounds, I subsequently discovered) and a hideous, phallic-shaped statuette, the Malta Cultural Award.

'Why didn't you wake me before you left the hotel this morning?' I asked him.

'I came to your room, but you weren't there, so I assumed you'd gone on without me. But you weren't at the ceremony, so I improvised an excuse for you, but then I began to be worried. I thought you might have been kidnapped by that taxi driver last night.'

'Perhaps I was. I don't remember a thing. Where am I now? Whose room is this?'

'It's an otherwise unoccupied room,' Ian told me. 'When I came back after collecting the prize, I insisted that the hotel people search for you. Then the night porter remembered you coming in very late last night. You must have given him the wrong room number, and he handed over the key you asked for. You staggered in here and passed out, I suppose.'

And that is how I failed to attend the Malta Cultural Award ceremony in the Palace of the Grand Masters, 'in the presence of the highest authorities of the State, Diplomatic Corps, economic leaders and the international press corps'. Ian and I made it to the Gala Dinner on the Saturday evening, but opted out of lunch with the Ministry of Education and Culture on Sunday, as well as a party given by the Governor-General. Instead, we decided to spend the day on the beach. But we had to take a taxi to the other end of the island to find a sandy beach, on which we immediately fell asleep, only to be awakened by having sand kicked in our faces by British Royal Navy ratings playing football. 'Christ,' Ian muttered, 'we might as well have gone to Blackpool for the weekend.'

Russell Davies Cartoon: Ian as Hamlet

Michael Fried

Early Days With Ian Hamilton

I'm not at all certain what a contribution by me to a Festschrift for Ian Hamilton ought to consist in. But looking at the list of contributors it occurred to me that I might be the person in this volume whose friendship with Ian goes back earliest. So I shall say something, no doubt not all that might be said, about early days.

I met Ian during my first year at Oxford, 1959-60. We were both regulars at the Oxford Poetry Society and Ian was an officer: Vice-President (I think) in 1959-60, and President (I think) in l960-61. I had better state right off that I loathed Oxford from the moment I arrived (I mean that literally: it still amazes me that I stepped off the bus that deposited our crew of American Rhodes Scholars on the High or wherever, took one look around, and detested all I saw). My recollection is that Ian and I began to get to know each other in my second year (his third), by which time it had become clear to me that I wasn't reading for any sort of degree but rather was avoiding the American draft while trying to figure out what to do with my life besides writing poems. I liked Ian from the first, partly because of his sense of humour, which was like nothing else I had ever encountered (that remains true to this day), partly because he seemed almost as alienated from Oxford as I was. I see now that my sense of his alienation must have been largely a matter of projection, which is to say that Ian couldn't have been in the perpetual state of fury and frustration that I was and still have managed to function at all. But I loved his brilliant commentaries on the idiocy and pretentiousness all around us, plus we shared an admiration for recent American poetry – above all Lowell's *Life Studies* but also Roethke's now underrated lyrics of the late 1950s, which I particularly valued. (I had been a student of

129

R P Blackmur's at Princeton, and arrived at Oxford a passionate advocate of the American modernist tradition.) We also had several long conversations about his hopes to attend graduate school in English in the States, a project that fell through once Ian learned that he had got a Third in Schools (is that how one says this?). Actually for years afterwards – until a recent exchange with Ian – I believed that he had got a Fourth, and was abashed to learn that he hadn't (I had taken derived pride in so unquestioned a distinction). Some time during my second year (I think) Ian edited and published a little magazine, *Tomorrow*. I have a memory of standing with him near Carfax and turning through an issue (can there have been just one?), which included a poem by him – which I can't quite recall. The truth is that although I counted him among my English friends, I didn't yet fully appreciate who and what he was.

That changed forever when Ian showed me the first group of poems he wrote that would eventually be published in *The Visit*. Again, my memory of the event is uncertain; it took place in London, where I had moved after leaving Oxford, either early summer or, more likely, early fall 1961. In any case, I instantly recognized that he had broken through to something remarkable and told him so. On that occasion too I showed him five or six poems that I had recently written, and both of us were struck by certain similarities of form and approach between his pieces and mine; simply put, we were both writing short intense lyric poems based on personal experience. I think it's fair to say that both of us were cheered by an unexpected sense of poetic brotherhood. But I shouldn't claim to speak for Ian. For myself then: starting that afternoon and continuing to the present moment, Ian has been a cardinal fact of my consciousness, the poet of my generation whose work I admire most, am most moved by, most deeply believe in.

Some time afterward Ian convened a meeting in a Greek restaurant on Tottenham Court Road with me, Colin Falck (with whom I was sharing an apartment and who was in the process of leaving philosophy for poetry), and John Fuller (whom Ian had known at Oxford), to discuss the founding of a new magazine of poetry and criticism to be called *The Review*. I was all for this, though I tried to convince Ian that the title was a mistake. He was immovable (this was not the last time I found him so), and in the long run was proved right. The first issue appeared in April/May 1962 and featured a long and intelligent discussion between A Alvarez and Donald Davie as well as poems by Alvarez, Davie, Zbigniew Herbert, Peter Redgrove, Roy Fuller, Vladimir Mayakovsky, and myself; it also marked the first appearance in print of the critic 'Edward Pygge', whose scathing and hilarious commentaries on contemporary writers had much in common with some of Ian's diabolically funny riffs on the same themes. Issues appeared at least four times a year (as I remember), a stupendous achievement in view of the fact that in crucial respects, including finances, *The Review* was a one-man show.

With a scrupulousness that seemed to me excessive, Ian declined to publish his own poems in the magazine, though in 1964 there appeared in place of issue no.13 three pamphlets of poems, among them his *Pretending Not to Sleep*. I have it on my desk as I write this, with its pea-green lettering on the white cover (Ian claimed that colour for himself, as if anyone else would have wanted it!) and its fourteen extraordinary poems including 'The Storm,' 'Birthday Poem,' 'Last Illness,' 'Pretending Not to Sleep,' and 'Poem (To G).' The last of these reads:

Ah, listen now
Each breath more temperate, more kind
More close to death.
Sleep on
And listen to these words
Faintly, and with a tentative alarm,
Refuse to waken you.

131

What could be more moving, more musical, more beautiful? The dedication of that poem to Gisela, Ian's first wife, leads me to add that she is a distinct and special presence in many of his finest poems of the 1960s. No doubt Ian would have written equally moving poems had they never met; but they did meet and become a couple (and marry, and have a son), and his work was forever touched by the experience.

At the end of the summer of 1962 I returned to the USA to begin graduate work in art history at Harvard, and in the years since then I have seen Ian only intermittently, almost always on visits to London. On one such visit in the 1970s, after a longer interval than usual, we had a brief lunch that led me during the weeks that followed to write a poem called 'Pain' (the office it refers to was of course the one Ian occupied for years at 11 Greek Street):

Pain

They told me you had lost all your hair
And then that it had grown back gray
But when I finally saw you
It was merely downy, like a young rabbit's.

Your eyes were red of course
And your fingers trembled as always
But you looked in robust health nonetheless.
Naturally when I said this you were offended

And lit up yet another high-tar cigarette
To crucify the already unbreathable atmosphere
In that infamous office hung with effigies of poets.
Now your latest communication

Reaches me via this week's *Times Literary Supplement* –
Your usual dozen perfect lines,
A dozen eyedropper drops of cloudless pain
Which taken internally would surely kill.

from *To the Center of the Earth* (New York:
Farrar, Straus and Giroux, 1994)

Some time after I wrote that poem Ian visited America, I
think in connection with his work on J D Salinger, and I showed
it to him. At that time line 9 read: 'And lit up yet another cigarette'; I
was dissatisfied with it because I knew something more, an adjective
modifying 'cigarette', was needed, but for the life of me I couldn't
figure out what it should be. It took Ian fifteen seconds to come
up with 'high-tar'.

Incident at St Denis

Out near the left corner post, Miller, with characteristic hauteur, beat Ungaretti and launched the cross without even looking inward. Hamilton, moving in at top speed from right of centre, instantly calculated where he would have to be to intercept it. There were two Italians he would need to outrun, Montale and Quasimodo. Both were fast, but they were facing the wrong way. With his unrivalled footballing brain, Hamilton knew already that he would get there. The problem would be to strike the ball into a space that the Italian goalkeeper, Pasolini, was already moving fast to close down. With only thirty seconds left before the whistle, and the score level at 5–all, this last, slim, desperate chance could decide the World Cup in England's favour. It was all down to Hamilton. He had scored all five of England's goals, three of them from his famous upside-down overhead backward somersault bicycle kick, but if he missed this one he would not be forgiven. Experience would help. He and Miller had been in the front line of the England squad since Moore, Charlton and the rest had helped them to that first World Cup success – the prelude to so many others – at Wembley in 1966. On that occasion, too, a typically sly pass by Miller to Hamilton's unerring right foot had clinched the issue. That had been a while ago, of course: Hamilton would be the first to admit it. Miller never admitted anything, but even he, if threatened with a cocked automatic, would concede between clenched teeth that he might no longer be quite capable of the ninety-yard diagonal run that had left Beckenbauer floundering before the back-flick to Hamilton had yielded the decider. Still, that was the great thing about this game. You might lose the odd tiny fraction of a mile per hour for each decade at the top, but you made up for it in wisdom, guile, grit and craft.

As Hamilton, after feinting to Montale's left, hurdled over the Italian's hacking right leg, his mind played its familiar trick of expanding, for a crucial split second, into another time, another place, another life. For strangely enough, this man, who ranked amongst the nonpareils of football ('There is another Pelé called Maradonna', Brian Glanville had once written, 'and there is another George Best called Paul Gascoigne, but there is no other Hamilton') was cursed, or blessed, with an imagination that furnished him with a whole separate existence. In his dreams, which came upon him most intensely when he was awake, and were at their most luxuriant in moments of professional footballing crisis, he was a poet, critic, editor, biographer and all-round man of letters. Unlike most imagined lives, his was full of vivid detail. He did not just vaguely dream of being a poet. There were actual poems, composed instantaneously in his head even as it was still ringing with the impact of the opposing goalkeeper's drop-kick clearance sent back past that stunned individual into the top corner of the net at seventy miles an hour. It was happening now.

> In the corner of my eye
> You move to the kitchen.
> Why do I not tell you
> That I ate the last bran flakes
> During the night?

It was the first stanza of a new poem which he knew would complete itself in the next few seconds of furious physical action. Such compositions – terse, acerbic, pregnant with angst, armoured to the core against any probe for sentimentality – lay at the heart of his early and still recurring conjured persona as the hard young literary guru of Soho. The same scenario would replay itself endlessly in his mind at moments like this. In his imagination, he entered once again the decrepit pub in Greek Street. The grand name he had invented for this sticky-carpeted dive, The Pillars of Hercules, was designed to create an ironic distance from its squalor. The place fell silent as he strode slowly in, dressed in black like Doc Holliday breasting the swinging saloon doors of Tombstone. Gripped in his lethal right hand were the galleys of his little magazine, *The Review*, the rarely appearing periodical in which established poetic reputations were riddled and left for dead. Propped against the bar, his worshipping acolytes tried unsuccessfully to look casual as they sensed his entrance. Which of them would be next for the bullet? Which of them would next discover that no amount of loudly professed loyalty was proof against the unswerving integrity of their chosen editor? Once again he bathed in the furtive glance of fear, even as now, in real life, he saw apprehension in the eyes of the Argentine fullback, Borges, the only man he had left to beat before he faced their legendary goalkeeper Sabato, who was already on his way out to narrow the angle. Borges was practically sideways in mid-air, launching a tackle designed to cut Hamilton's lithely muscled legs from under him. He could let it happen, get the penalty, and finish the match that way. The second stanza flashed into his head.

> Perhaps because
> I need your disappointment
> To equal mine. The hallway
> Is full to waist level
> With buff envelopes.

The poem was already half done. Soon it would finish itself, just as he would finish this goal. A goal it would have to be: a penalty was the coward's way. It wasn't his style. His style was integrity, and that meant what he must do now: beat the tackle with all the skills he had first developed as a youth in those endless hours of kicking a crushed tin can through his letterbox while being attacked by the family dog, and had gone on honing through hundreds of First Division and international matches in which the opposing backs had dedicated themselves to marking him out of the game. With a delicacy and precision made doubly incredible by the speed at which he was travelling, he nudged the ball through the space left under the horizontal body of the Brazilian fullback, de Moraes, and launched himself over it as the crowd's continuous roar rose to an orgiastic frenzy. Hamil-TON! Hamil-TON! It got boring sometimes, all that adoration.

He was still in mid-air when he began to calculate the options available to the rapidly advancing goalkeeper, Cabral. Here once again, if it were needed, was startling evidence of Hamilton's greatest single gift: the ability to compute possible trajectories even while his finely-tuned physical capacity was fully committed to the action of the present instant. ('If the photon-stream of the Hamiltonesque footballing mode can best be resolved through a lens which owes more to Heidegger than to Heisenberg,' George Steiner had once written, 'perhaps the crux of our appreciation lies in the very synchronicity of *spurlos* intellection and breath-bereaving *Affekt* which we, simultaneously deceived and undeceived, are delightedly aware unites us in belief even at the moment when we are unable to believe our eyes.') De Moraes was already behind, flailing helpless on the turf, automatically signalling innocence to the referee for a foul which he had not managed to commit. Hamilton descended to rejoin the ball as Cabral checked his own headlong rush and distributed his weight evenly to both feet, ready to launch himself in whichever direction the hurtling Hamilton might choose to strike. It was the supreme moment of decision.

> As I forge through them
> To the front door,
> It sounds like cereal being eaten
> Without milk.

Hamilton had nobody left to beat except the Norwegian goalkeeper, Ibsen. It would not be easy. Ibsen stood ready to go either way. But Hamilton the footballer could read an opponent's intentions in the same way that, in his imagined role as Hamilton the literary biographer, he could read the complex creative psychology of his chosen subject. Just as, in his reveries, he had penetrated to the central motivation of Robert Lowell's paranoia and J D Salinger's strange reluctance to offer himself up for questioning, so now, in reality, he infallibly analysed the Scandinavian's notorious coiled-spring poise. The bacchantic tumult of the crowd was not enough to muffle the crack of a heavy-calibre rifle shot as Hamilton struck the ball with all his force to his opponent's right while imparting to it, with a long-practised flexing of the foot, the special spin that would curl it to the left. Even as he did so, Hamilton was looking into the grandstand out of the corner of his eye. Kate was there, taking a day off from filming *Titanic II*. Jennifer and Courteney were on either side of her: production of *Friends* had been suspended for a day at their insistence. Julia was only just arriving, typically: later on she would probably babble that the private jet from Los Angeles had run short of fuel. He was getting sick of Julia's excuses. If she kept that up, her suite in the women's wing at his chateau on the Loire (*Hello!* had done a special supplement, back in the days when Sigourney and Michelle were still in residence) might just have to be reassigned to young Gwyneth, who God knows had put in enough requests. Even now, with all the women on their feet cheering, Gwyneth looked the most ecstatic. Good girl. Hamilton was resolving to reward her with a new Porsche even as Ibsen read the trick, reversed direction in mid-air, and got a hand to the ball.

Now you have the milk
But without cereal.
Tough break.
Let's call it a draw.

The poem was completed but the goal was not. The German goalkeeper, Festschrift, had got a hand to the ball but of course he couldn't hold it. Hamilton's shot, moving at only just below the speed of sound, had been too powerful. Hamilton knew what must happen next. He had planned it all along. The only chance with Festschrift was to get him with the second bite of the cherry, not the first. The ball rebounded in a high arc. From behind, the fullbacks Enzensburger and Grass had recovered fast and were moving in. Hamilton was upside down in mid-air when he glanced into the stands and saw Julia, Jennifer, Kate, Courteney and Gwyneth all clutching their distorted faces in horror at the prospect of his missing this most vital of all goals. But he was not going to miss. He never missed with the upside-down overhead backward somersault bicycle kick with the special spin. 'Ach, du Schweinhund Hamilton mit deine magische talent!' screamed Festschrift as the ball streaked past him into the net.

Slackjawed with awe, the referee finally remembered himself and blew the whistle. A hundred thousand people were shouting too loudly to hear it. Nor could the object of their adulation. But he didn't need to. He knew the job was done. On his hands and knees, suddenly weary, Hamilton glanced towards the grandstand and realised at last why Julia had arrived late. He had forgotten but the girls had not. Julia had brought the cake. They were all lighting the candles.

Damned pity it took such a long time, but there was a lot more football in him yet.

Songs Among The Ruins

Matthew Arnold, in his occasionally almost optimistic mode as a social critic, could see a promising future for poetry arising out of the progressive crumbling of our traditional religious beliefs. In his more heartfelt and instinctive role as a poet, he could rise to little more than disillusion or despair. The possibilities of survival for the human spirit had already been diminished to the realm of the immediate and the personal, and the only hope worth clinging to was that we might 'be true to one another' while the ignorant armies clashed by night in the poetically-abandoned world of history.

One of the first unforgettable phrases I remember hearing from Ian after meeting him early in 1962 (we had been introduced by Michael Fried – these were the personal soundings-out and ground-clearings that somehow established the rather *macho* critical identity of *The Review*) – was 'the voice of remorseless optimism'. When I had met him a good deal more, I saw how this brilliant and sardonic notion could work its way into almost any conversation or situation where Ian was present, whether it involved poetry, personal relationships, the thirtieth birthday of Jimmy Greaves, the availability of a girl at a neighbouring table, or the likelihood that a waiter would ever bring us the drinks we had ordered. When I began to talk this way in other people's company I found myself being branded as old-fashionedly cynical, but it now seems a *point de repère* (we had all read Eliot's early essays) of my own past that I see Ian so immovably there in it as a beacon of romantic restraint (you can only be restrained if you have some-thing to restrain) amid the surrounding unbridled enthusiasms. (How suggestive it now seems that Ian's last poetic merger before *The Review* should have been with Michael Horovitz, and how necessary to the Apollonian/Dionysian poetic geography of the period that it should have failed.) That enthusiasms should be bridled and actually ridden somewhere was for some of us a principle of art and of life, and Ian's graceful puritanism (one thinks of Orwell, perhaps, but also of the Eliot of 'La Figlia che Piange', the carapace of intellect protecting the soft romantic centre; even perhaps of Wilde, and of the necessity that all things, including living, if one has the money for it, should be done with style) was often a reassuringly fixed point in a beguilingly uncharted cultural landscape. There were those who wondered what it was that Ian actually *was* restraining, but they were persons of coarse-grained sensibility unlike ourselves, who did not write poetry or understand it, and they did not need to be reckoned with.

It was several years and a stage or two in my own education later that I began to see Ian as Arnoldian. After grappling uncertainly with modern French Marxism (Charles Taylor had made me feel I should stay with it, Isaiah Berlin that I probably shouldn't) I had begun to suffer from the rift between all these theory-laden (and academically respectable) prognostications and my inwardly gloomier romantic longings. The spiritual disaster that this seemed to be shaping up for me was more that of John Stuart Mill than of anyone else (and I had already *read* Wordsworth), but it was certainly mid-nineteenth century. Having been persuaded long before by Michael Fried that I could not hold all of these things together Auden-fashion in a single poetry, I was ready enough to be persuaded by Ian that they should simply be allowed to fall apart. I relaxed with relief into 'Dover Beach' as a poetic testament, and even pointed out to Ian that he had plagiarized the fourth line of it in his own poem 'Trucks'. How far and by what chemistry, all of this led Ian to take me on as his associate editor on *The Review* perhaps no one could now say (there was a good deal of sheer practicality in it), but the sense of a shared sensibility where almost nothing in poetry had to be argued about and almost everything could be placed and settled by an allusive phrase or two (an upmarket version of plain old Sixties inarticulateness, perhaps, but probably the kind of thing that always lies behind the births of movements) was an enormous editorial convenience. Not that Ian had many inclinations towards democratic discussions of editorial matters anyway: *The Review*, despite its showpiece editorial board (which never once met in plenary session), was Ian's personal creation (and intellectual arena, and career project, and financial nemesis), and contributions by others were always contributions to something – a planned special issue, a future battle to be fought, the direction of the magazine itself – that was already in existence and was probably heading somewhere. But if there were to be two editors, and if both were actually to do something, it was convenient, given the rather fascistic editorial instincts of both, that there should be an uncanny overlap of sensibility. This was the time when we would send postcards to each other addressed to 'Wordsworth' (Ian was Wordsworth) or 'Coleridge', sometimes even from Nether Stowey or Dove Cottage, and when we were thinking almost consciously about how we could take poetry back to *Lyrical Ballads* and somehow forwards again from there into a real lyrical future.

The uncanny overlap of sensibility was probably put to its biggest test with the compilation of our anthology *Poems Since 1900*. This was an idea we had talked about throughout the later years of *The Review* – it always seemed that it *should* be easy to do – but which finally came to publication (Wordsworthian-Coleridgean fallings-out having played a certain part in the delay) only in 1975. Here, as so often, we almost never met along the way to discuss the project, however much we met for other reasons, but when we finally compared our separately-compiled lists there turned out to be a seventy-five per cent overlap in our choices of poems (the diverging twenty-five per cent was at least partly the result of our division of reading labour rather than of actual critical disagreement). Nor was there any committee work when it came to the writing of the preface: I wrote the text myself, and Ian cut out various bits of it and inserted a few sentences, and we left it at that. It could just as easily have been the other way round. Our meetings at this time took place in Ian's Westbourne Terrace flat, my own permanently half-renovated Camden house being afflicted by what Ian called 'delicately informal decor' (plaster rubble on many of the floors), but I remember bringing the largest giant sunflower from our half-renovated garden and leaving it in a pot on Ian's doorstep: this many-headed Blakean symbol presided over our final poem-choosings (and perhaps our rather shaky personal lives) for several weeks. Another aspect of this mystically-unified editorial hard-nosedness could sometimes be seen in the back pages of *The Review*, especially in its later years. The satirist 'Edward Pygge,' originally and most of the time Ian himself, eventually came to embrace several aliases, and his ruthlessness and anonymity had a powerful strategic impact in the poetic wars of the day. (It could sometimes be difficult to reclaim one's intellectual property later: some of my own parodies – William Carlos Williams, Robert Bly, Charles Tomlinson – were routinely attributed to Ian by innocently- intentioned anthologists, and there must be other contributory trouble-makers who had the same experience.)

When *The Review* became *The New Review,* Ian's status as a poetic – and now more generally literary – pundit and arbiter became entrenched in a largish organization that faithfully worked for him. As the poetry editor of this metropolitan outfit I was given an entirely free hand apart from the occasional interposition of a poem by some poet of the moment whom it was politically important not to reject. This was really a part of *The Review*'s growing-up – and of course one of the things that brought accusations of sell-out by various dedicated but more hole-and-corner purists. One began to think in terms of 'broadly'. *The New Review* was broadly, despite its necessary compromises, a voice for some kind of attempted bringing-over of the exquisitely-tuned and verse-based sensibility of the old *Review* into the wider world of literature and culture at large. Whether this could really be done at all was a question that was never quite explicitly faced. *The New Review* was eventually destroyed – a victim of cultural committee wars – by a purportedly more democratic faction which saw Arts Council money as having been disproportionately hijacked by an enterprise that was elitist in its spirit and which sold very few copies of its magazine on the streets. Give or take a grudge or two either way, this was a fair enough account. In effect Ian had done the best that he could have done in the circumstances, which was to get as much public money for as long as he could in order to give some readers some elitist writing that they needed to get and before the ignorant armies took over. Other snouts in the trough would produce other kinds of literature. Broadly, the rise and fall of *The New Review* now seems a prefiguring of the grander cultural wars that have brought the whole future of literature into question – has there been a 'death of literature'? etc. – wherever literature is still written or read (or not, as the case may be). From this point onwards Ian would pull back from such public battlings and put his energies into writing books – sometimes about elitist writers.

And he would go on writing poems. It would be wrong to call Ian's attitude to the writing of poetry itself elitist – everything he has written is utterly accessible and readable (one can almost imagine it addressed to some secret, dreamed-of equivalent of Yeats's fisherman: 'Before I am old / I shall have written him one / Poem maybe as cold / And passionate as the dawn') – but his insistence on the highest craftsmanship at a time when the unshaven horsemen of populism were taking over poetry's outer provinces was an expression of cultural faith as well as of personal dedication. The poetry he has written, and has gone on writing, has been a poetry of immediate personal experiencing, most often of love, or of remembered and reflected-on personal relationships, and it has always been finely responsive to the interplay between ordinary everyday speech and the deeper rhythms of the English language itself – in particular its internalization of the iambic pentameter as a means of conveying some of our deepest feelings and apprehensions. With the possible exception of D H Lawrence, the only British poet to have taken the full impact of American free verse (a tradition that now stretches from Whitman to Plath) and to have carried it further in his own poetry is Ian Hamilton. The most delicate of the poems in *The Visit* (1970) show the results of this at their beautifully crafted best:

> The tall weeds trail their hair
> And spiral lazily
> Up from their barnacled black roots
> As if to touch
> (Though hardly caring)
> The light that polishes their quiet pool.
>
> 'Funeral'

Or:

> It's midnight
> And our silent house is listening
> To the last sounds of people going home.
> We lie beside our curtained window
> Wondering
> What makes them do it.
>
> 'Curfew'

Or:

> Four weathered gravestones tilt against the wall
> Of your Victorian asylum.
> Out of bounds, you kneel in the long grass
> Deciphering obliterated names:
> Old lunatics who died here.
>
> 'Memorial'

Or from his privately printed pamphlet *Returning* (1976):

> Look at it, I'd say to you
> If you were here: it is a sign
> Of what is brief, and lonely
> And in love.
> But you are gone and so I'll call it wise:
> A patient breath, an eye, a rose
> That opens up too easily and dies
>   'Rose'

Apart from the guest-incursions of the early Eliot (soon to be thrown off as an alien graft by the native tradition), British poetry has nothing else to show like this. In his most recent poems, as in 'The Garden' (*Steps*, Cargo 1997), Hamilton takes new risks by moving further away from the stress-of-some-emotion immediacy of natural speech, but the tension between natural speech and the deeper rhythms of the language (a tension perhaps partly derived from Robert Frost, whom he perceptively edited) continues to be there:

> The vegetation's rank, I'll grant you that,
> The weeds well out of order, shoulder-high
> And too complacently deranged. The trees
> Ought not to scrape your face, your hands, your hair
> Nor so haphazardly swarm upwards to impede
> The sunlit air you say you need to breathe
> In summertime.

With his continued insistence on close-at-hand personal experience for his subject matter Hamilton almost unavoidably finds himself being classified as a 'confessional' poet (although even the most confessional poet presents his experience as symbolic, his sufferings as exemplary for the rest of us, if he is a poet at all), and his debt to poets like Robert Lowell or Sylvia Plath have always been freely acknowledged and obvious. As far as historical or global matters or the behaviours of ignorant armies are concerned, the Hamiltonian method has always been to treat them only as they impinge on our personal lives, or else not to treat them at all. In 'Newscast', the world-historical events are actually mediated by the media, and

> The Vietnam war drags on
> In one corner of our living room

rather than being bardically preached about in the protest-poetry manner of the day. In his contempt for all suggestions of the bardic and in his confining of his poetry to a lyricism of personal things (hands, hair – nothing further away than a landscape), Hamilton has staked out a defiant critical position within his own actual poems. One critic astutely spoke of *The Review*'s most common style of poetry as 'critical minimalism'. In its defensive self-restriction to such things as hands or hair or landscapes the style might now strike us as minimal almost to the point of self-defeat – virtually any personal experience thus conveyed must carry with it something of the 'mournful cosmic last resort' quality that Anthony Hecht satirized in 'The Dover Bitch' – but in its insight into everything that has threatened to obliterate a true poetry of experiencing in the mid-to-late twentieth century it could hardly be considered too critical.

An extreme reaction against such tight-reined poetic prescriptiveness was almost bound to have followed. Hamilton himself has said (in an interview in the Oxford magazine *The Reader*, reprinted in *Poetry Review*):

I think I could have probably predicted – and perhaps even

did – the Martian phenomenon that came after the kind of stuff I was encouraging in *The Review* and *The New Review* ... It got narrower and narrower in its focus; too narrow in the end ... Then you might have predicted a resurgence of political poetry. The gulf between the idea of poetry as intensely personal and the idea of poetry as a political instrument had become vast.

Something, all of a sudden, was pushing personal poetry to the side of its own life, and it was not entirely clear in all cases that what was pushing it was a real or worthwhile kind of poetry at all. In the introduction to his *Oxford Companion to Twentieth-Century Poetry in English* (1994) Hamilton is (necessarily no doubt) diplomatic about all the different 'poetries' that the English-speaking world now contains. Three years later (in the interview quoted above) he comes out more explicitly and all but dismisses some of the most recent goings-on on the British poetic scene:

> Most of what is out there today isn't really poetry... It might be a form of writing that is engaging and sharp and entertaining, but it is not poetry. It's important to make these distinctions; every line doesn't count, every word hasn't been chosen carefully, it doesn't have any structure; there's no reason why this line is broken and that line is not...

When it comes to what poetry *is* he reminds us that

> difficult, complex poetry has become a minority art. There are still things in the best poems that cannot be found in any other form of literary expression. And it's those things which are to do with the shapes and sounds of true poetry. They are to do with concentration and a strange combination of intense feeling and icily controlled craftsmanship.

Most of today's poets do not even seem to have bothered to read the poetry of the tradition at all:

> Today, I think many poems are being written by people who have no poetry in their heads ... they don't know where they are when you present them with a poem by Hardy or Frost. They're not prepared for the immediate sense of difficulty or strangeness because they have no background in poetry. If it dosen't hit them in the face or make them laugh it has no value for them.

– or if it matters how it looks on the page as opposed to how it sounds in the auditorium, he might have added. Hamilton is surely right that it no longer seems normal (as it did to Ian or to Michael Fried or to myself) that a poet should have many hundreds of lines of poetry in his head (the best of 'the best that is known and thought', perhaps) – exactly remembered, but almost never consciously learned – as a badge of admission to being a poet at all.

When a real poetic history of our period comes to be written these perceptions may all come to seem more obvious and less extreme than they seem now. In committing himself to critical or biographical writing rather than striving officiously to keep poetry alive in the public world Hamilton has probably found the best use for his own energies, but poetry in general, and even the whole of literature, has meanwhile come to seem to lie under an ever more drastic and perhaps even terminal cultural threat. Where a critic like Lionel Trilling could hold on (as F R Leavis had held on) to the idea of literature as culturally central and even a spiritual healing power, recent intellectual fashions (Marxism, post-structuralism) have generally been thought to have de-centred the literary text and to have stripped it of its once-numinous authority: the old romantic-modernist idea of the poem as a verbal icon or a well-wrought urn has rather few adherents today. Alvin Kernan, in

The Death of Literature (1990), can even wonder if literature has a future at all. When we factor into this all-pervading literary breakdown the ever more widely burgeoning power of 'digital communication', the poet or the literary critic might easily enough begin to think of himself as an entirely irrelevant and powerless stone-age survival. Perhaps little of all this will have come as a surprise to Hamilton, who has for a long time been negotiating his personal retreat from relevance, and whose first essay in his first collection of essays *A Poetry Chronicle* (1973) was already called 'Songs Among the Ruins'. Standing at the end of a long line of Romantic critics since Coleridge he has had the bleakest landscape of all to face.

In *The Gutenberg Elegies* (1994) Sven Birkerts weighs up the prospects for literature and for the human psyche in the face of 'circuit-driven mass culture', and notes 'the progressive atrophy of all that defines us as creatures of spirit'. But he also sees a flicker of hope:

> If we are wired for meaning, and if psyche is a closed system – two big ifs – then it follows, as Freud would agree, that repressed elements return ... We witnessed one such blast in the 60s ... The 1960s were only incidentally about drugs or sexual experimentation or rock and roll – these were epiphenomena. They were about protest ... Slowly, steadily, we may see the pressure build, and with it the awareness in individuals of a vacancy at the subjective core ... And when the crisis does come, no chip or screen will have a solution for it. It will flash forth as an insistent need, a soul craving, and nothing binary will suffice.

The human spirit may rise up against its repression, this hope tells us, and demand a reunification with its own body rather than with the delights of 'virtual reality' or the circuits of a mainframe computer. With his fierce loyalty to a poetry of bodily presence (and a refusenik's loyalty to his manual typewriter) Ian Hamilton may have shown us something of a way forward from our impending crisis rather than a way back. If the return of the repressed begins to happen, if we feel a need for a saving poetry of physical immediacies that can be intimately trusted, the kind of poetry he has written and endorsed may be a place for us to start out from again: a poetry not of ego-flourishing or of bardic posturing or of verbal cleverness, but of a quiet and reverential humility before the real. With his by-now-serene indifference to his own bodily welfare Hamilton may not perhaps be counting on being around when any such revival occurs. Perhaps it will take a thousand years anyway. Robinson Jeffers, the twentieth century's most eloquent poetic pessimist, advised us to 'Look to it: prepare for the long winter: spring is far off'. Heidegger, always seeing technology as our chief mode of 'forgetting of Being' but never living to see what our most recent technology would be capable of, thought it might all take a very long time. Those of us who have known Ian and loved him for his unflinchingly Hardyan 'full look at the worst' must honour him for the clarity of the hope he allows us to keep alive and for the signposts he has given us towards a habitable and human future. Perhaps – though this may be the voice of remorseless optimism – it could even happen sooner rather than later.

Set in Bembo by
Cargo Press

Cargo Poetry

~

John Greening

Ian Hamilton

David Harsent

Derrek Hines

Alice Kavounas

Judith Kazantzis

Jon Silkin

Goran Simić

Cargo Manifest available from
Cargo Press
Tregarne, Manaccan
Cornwall   TR12 6EW
UK